O'Hare to Boston Ma

USS Denver Benasai

9-93

MIDWEST LIVING®
Editor: Dan Kaercher
Managing Editor: Barbara Humeston
Art Director: Richard Michels
Food Editor: Diana McMillen
Senior Staff Editor: George Hendrix
Senior Writer: Barbara Briggs Morrow
Contributing Food Editor: Barbara Albrecht

Editorial Director: Doris M. Eby
Publishing Director: Adolph Auerbacher

Publisher: Tom E. Benson
Advertising Director: Lyle C.R. Landon

Magazine Group President: William T. Kerr

MEREDITH® **BOOKS**
President, Book Group: Joseph J. Ward
Vice President and Editorial Director: Elizabeth P. Rice

FAVORITE RECIPES FROM GREAT MIDWEST COOKS
Contributing Editors: Diana McMillen, Rosemary
   Hutchinson, Sharyl Heiken, Liz Woolever
Project Editor: Marsha Jahns
Designer: Lyne Neymeyer

Cover: Autumn in the village of Metamora, Indiana
   Apple Pie á la Mode (*see recipe, page 50*)

All of us at Meredith® Books are dedicated to providing you with the information and ideas you need to create tasty foods. We welcome your comments or suggestions. Write us at: Meredith® Books, Cookbook Editorial Department, LS-348, 1716 Locust St., Des Moines, IA 50309-3023.

Every recipe in *Favorite Recipes from Great Midwest Cooks* has been tested in the Meredith® Books Test Kitchen to assure that it is practical and reliable and meets our high standards of taste appeal. We guarantee your satisfaction with this book for as long as you own it.

If you would like to order additional copies of this book or copies of any of our other books for yourself or for gifts, call 1-800-678-2803 or check your local bookstore.

Favorite

RECIPES

from

GREAT MIDWEST

COOKS

by the editors of
MIDWEST LIVING®
magazine

MEREDITH® **BOOKS**
Des Moines

Contents

The Heartland

From majestic, weathered barns standing
watch over fields of corn and wheat . . . to
ore boats and grain barges parting the icy
waters of lakes and rivers . . . to the quiet,
tree-lined streets of county-seat towns and
soaring office towers gleaming in the summer
sun, the Midwest has it all. Diverse
landscapes, industries, people, cultures,

and customs give the 12 states in the center of our nation a character all their own.

This diversity and uniqueness shines in the foods of the Heartland. Whether they're devouring thick
wedges of flaky-crusted pie bursting with plump berries, feasting on succulent capon nestled in a pool of
delicate fresh tarragon sauce, or munching great ears of fresh-picked corn dripping with butter,

4

Midwesterners love good food. They believe that the
food on their tables speaks volumes about
who they are and where they've come from. They settle
only for the best.

So come with us on a gastronomic tour. We'll visit
Ohio, Michigan, Indiana, Wisconsin, Illinois,

Minnesota, Iowa, Kansas, Missouri, Nebraska, North Dakota, and South Dakota. We'll show you the way Midwesterners eat today. We'll introduce you to hospitable, inventive cooks who use the foods of the Heartland to create new combinations and taste sensations. We'll visit celebrations, state fairs, and festivals. Tour farms, orchards, and grain mills. Drop in at candy shops, bakeries, and butcher shops. And poke through some of the best markets in the Midwest. By the time we've covered it all, we think you'll agree that the cooking of the Midwest is like its people— honest, rich in tradition, diverse, exciting, and totally irresistible.

Each year from Ohio to Nebraska, and Missouri to Michigan, thousands throng to county and state fairs, cook-offs, and local festivals that celebrate the foods and cooking of the Heartland. In this chapter we'll take you to some of the best of these celebrations. First, come with us to the state fair. Indiana, Illinois, and Iowa will be showing off their ribbon-winning cooks. There, you can judge for yourself which entries are the best pies, ice creams, and breads. Then, in Wisconsin, let us show you around Eagle River's Cranberry Fest. You'll learn how cranberries are harvested and taste what wonderful things good cooks can do with them. And finally, stop with us at the National Sweet Corn Festival in Hoopeston, Illinois, and experience one of the largest corn celebrations ever. We guarantee you'll enjoy all of the goings-on as much as the great eating.

Celebrations

Blue Ribbon Recipes

Come to where corn dogs and cotton candy make your mouth water, where midway lights spangle the sky, and where city and country folks celebrate state-fair treasures—soccer-ball-size tomatoes to dazzling quilts and sleek steers. Midwest cooks will be vying for blue-ribbon glory. We'll meet a few and sample their recipes.

Indiana State Fair

The countdown is on, as the best Hoosier bakers make a beeline for the Home and Family Arts Building to sign in before the 11:30 a.m. deadline. It's "pie day" at the Indiana State Fair.

For Helen Rushton of Greenfield and her daughter Mary Alice Collins of Markleville, the routine never changes. Helen arrives early, and with the help of her husband Ovie and her homemade wooden pie crates, checks in more than a dozen fresh home-baked pies—an assortment ranging from gooseberry to blackberry and apricot.

Then, Helen waits curbside, anxiously checking her wristwatch.

State fair time is baking time for Hoosiers Mary Alice Collins and her mother Helen Rushton. They insist it's the crust judges notice first.

"It never fails. Mary Alice always is last," she explains, smiling patiently.

With three minutes to spare, Helen and Ovie spot Mary Alice and her husband Darl cruising in their van through the fair's front gates. The van pulls up to the curb, the doors fly open, and Mary Alice—a pie in each hand—makes a spirited 50-yard dash to the sign-in desk. (If she gets just one pie there by the deadline, she's permitted to enter all her pies.) "That's living dangerously," says Helen, with a motherly sigh of relief.

PIES BY THE DOZENS

This year, Helen says she's slowing down. "After all, I'm in my eighties, so I only entered about a dozen pies." But Mary Alice, a real go-getter, continues the family's prolific pie-making tradition; she enters 22 of her pies.

All except one of her pies make the 30-mile journey from her home to the fairgrounds in good shape. A sudden stop in traffic sent the banana-cream pie's meringue sliding—after the filling stopped.

But Darl doesn't seem too disappointed. "Oh, well," he says, hungrily sizing up the disheveled pie.

Although Mary Alice majored in home economics at Purdue University, she confides, "I learned how to bake pies at my mother's side in the kitchen." That's where she gleaned the tips and techniques for success, like baking pies on the lower rack of the oven, sprinkling sugar on the top crusts of fruit pies for a

continued

delicacy's smooth creaminess comes from the hand-cranking effort. And they must be right. The McFarlands have claimed the blue ribbons in ice cream four times.

"We like to have our ice cream ready a couple hours before judging," says Joy, layering crushed ice and a few handfuls of rock salt around the frosty metal canister. David packs the ice snug with a metal rod, then covers the canister so the ice cream will get firm and its flavor will ripen.

COUNSEL FROM
HOMETOWN FANS

The new flavor ideas of this ambitious Ellston, Iowa, farm couple don't come from trips to Baskin-Robbins. (David says he's only eaten

golden finish after baking, and rolling out extra-thin piecrusts.

Mother and daughter share their pie-making secrets, but they also love the healthy state-fair competition. As Helen explains, "Sometimes I win; sometimes she wins."

200 BLUE RIBBONS
AND STILL COUNTING

Both women enter almost every kind of pie you can imagine, from oatmeal (they call it "poor-man's pecan") to chocolate cream, chess, pineapple, and "do-your-own-thing."

Over the years, the mother-and-daughter team has collected hundreds of awards and ribbons. "Just this morning," Helen says, "I opened a shoe box full of ribbons and counted almost 200." Along with acting as official pie carriers, Ovie and Darl share more important positions, as discerning taste testers for their spouses' prospective pie

entries. When polled about their favorite kinds of pies, without argument, the husbands concur, "We like two kinds—hot and cold."

J oy and David McFarland take turns cranking their White Mountain ice cream maker. Swirling around inside is their best hope for a blue ribbon in the ice cream division—cherry cobbler. The August sun heats the pavement around them on the concourse outside the Iowa State Fair's Family Center.

Most of the fair's ice cream entrants chose electric freezers. Not Joy and David. They insist that their

Iowa State Fair

Illinois State Fair

ice cream there four times.) "We don't pay attention to what everybody else is doing. We make what we think we'll like," says Joy.

Their cherry-cobbler ice cream (see recipe, page 18) was born as Joy sat on the basement steps. She noticed the canned pie cherries on a shelf: "I said, 'Wow! How about cherry-cobbler ice cream!' "

After they perfect the proportions of ingredients, the easy-to-know young couple lug their ice creams to local get-togethers, like the potluck suppers at the United Methodist

Church in nearby Arispe, for the true test. "We have a big audience down home that we try things out on," says David. "They don't mind that we use them as guinea pigs."

"I've had lots of experience eating ice cream," smiles David through his handlebar mustache. "I grew up on a dairy farm, and we raised guernseys. We used the cream from milk to make ice cream."

TIME OUT FOR THE FAIR

Almost every day of the fair, Joy and daughter Landi get up early and make the two-hour drive north to Des Moines. David forgoes his farm work to spend a couple of days at the fair (he's always there for the ice cream making and judging).

"The first time we entered our ice cream and won, we were blown away," laughs Joy, who credits that success to her husband. "His taster is better than mine. He's supercritical."

Even before this year's fair draws to a close, you'll probably see the McFarlands and one of their three White Mountain ice cream makers on the front porch of their white farmhouse. They're cranking up some new flavors for next year's competition.

**F**aith Mikita claims anyone can fit bread making into their schedule. She should know. She buys 20 pounds of flour for her doughy hobby every week, and she's been carting home state-fair blue ribbons

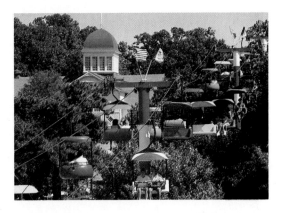

in bread making for 10 years now. In fact, before Faith joined the ranks of state-fair winners, she took so many prizes at the county fair that officials asked her to retire from the baking competition.

A modest, grandmotherly 60-something, Faith also teaches a bread-making class in her home. Her proudest protégé is her son Myron, who started entering state-fair competitions in 1982. Faith helped him develop a filled yeast-bread recipe called Raisin-Lovers' Surprise Loaves (see recipe, pages 16–17) that he prepared on stage at the Illinois State Fair and won fourth place.

The next year, Myron took first place with his sunburst-shaped coffee cake (see recipe, page 16). He's the first man ever to become a grand champion in the bread-making cook-off at the Illinois State Fair.

Rye breads are Myron's specialties. "They're hearty," he says. Myron, now a high-school band director in Gilbertville, Iowa, claims bread making came easy for him. "I had Mom to watch," he smiles. "If I ever had any questions, the answers always were right there."

BREAD-MAKING COOPERATION

Today, Myron and Faith learn from each other. As she works with one of the many
continued

13

flours she uses, Faith explains that you can interrupt bread making at almost any time, refrigerate the dough, and then finish shaping and baking the loaves later on.

How long should you knead bread dough? "Until tiny bubbles or blisters appear," says Faith, who claims that her failures are her best teachers. "You can't put a time limit on kneading."

One bread-making trick Myron taught his mom was a new way to smooth a round loaf. Instead of pinching and folding it, he simply rolls it on the countertop. The loaf bakes perfectly. "If he baked as much as I do," Faith predicts, "I'm sure he'd surpass me."

When Myron travels to different universities to talk to fellow band instructors, Faith goes along and heads for the library on campus, where she devours the contents of college textbooks on bread making. "Bread making is an art based on a science," she insists.

BAKING AS THERAPY

After years of practice, Faith also considers making bread a form of therapy. "You've got to toss that bread dough in the air and slap it around," she says with a grin. "When the bread dough starts to get sticky, that's your cue to toss it in the air. That cools the dough."

At the beginning of all her classes, Faith admonishes would-be bread makers to fill their mixing bowls with love. "If they're empty," she says, "I tell my students to quit right now. If their bowls are full of love, the bread will turn out."

Faith Mikita passed along her baking know-how to son Myron, Jr. Now, they both win at the fair.

Best-Ever Raisin-Orange Bread

Faith Mikita smiles when she remembers the honors that went to this bread. It captured grand champion, best bread of show, and best bread of class in the 1982 Illinois State Fair.

5   to 5½ cups bread flour
2   packages active dry yeast
1   cup milk
½   cup sugar
½   cup butter
¼   cup water
1   orange peel, finely shredded
1   teaspoon ground ginger
1½ teaspoons salt
2   eggs (at room temperature)
1½ cups raisins
    Walnut Glaze (see recipe, page 17)

1. In a large mixer bowl, combine *2 cups* of the flour and the yeast.
2. In a saucepan, heat together milk, sugar, butter, water, orange peel, ginger, and salt just till warm (120°), stirring constantly. Add to flour mixture; add eggs. Beat on low speed for 30 seconds, scraping bowl. Beat on high speed for 3 minutes. Add raisins.
3. Using a spoon, stir in as much of the remaining flour as you can. On floured surface, knead in enough remaining flour to make a moderately stiff dough that's smooth and elastic (6 to 8 minutes). Shape into a ball and place in greased bowl; turn once.
4. Cover dough; let rise in warm place till doubled (about 1¼ hours). Punch down. Turn out onto a floured surface; knead 1 minute. Cover; let rest for 15 minutes. Divide into 2 portions. Press each into a flat oval (9x7 inches); fold in half. Pinch seam closed. Pat to fit 2 greased 8½x4½x2-inch loaf pans.

5. Place dough in prepared pans. Make three ¼-inch-deep diagonal slashes across top of each loaf. Cover with waxed paper; let rise in a warm place till doubled (¾ to 1 hour). Remove waxed paper and bake in a 375° oven for 45 to 50 minutes or till done. (Cover loaves with foil after 20 minutes to prevent overbrowning.) Remove from pans; cool on wire racks.
6. Spread Walnut Glaze over cooled loaves. Makes 2 loaves (32 servings).

Sunrise Serenade
Coffee Cake

Myron Mikita, Jr., uses a doughnut cutter to form his soft, artistic yeast bread into this sunny shape.

- 2½ to 3 cups all-purpose or unbleached flour
- 1 package active dry yeast
- 1 teaspoon baking powder
- ⅓ cup dairy sour cream
- ⅓ cup orange juice
- ¼ cup sugar
- ¼ cup butter or margarine
- 1 teaspoon salt
- 1 egg
- 1 teaspoon finely shredded orange peel
- ¼ cup raspberry, currant, cherry, or strawberry jelly
   Orange Glaze
- ¼ cup toasted sliced almonds

1. In a large mixer bowl, combine *1 cup* of the flour, the yeast, and the baking powder. In a saucepan, heat the sour cream, ⅓ cup orange juice, sugar, butter or margarine, and salt till very warm (120° to 130°) and butter is almost melted, stirring constantly.
2. Stir heated mixture into flour mixture. Add egg and orange peel. Beat with an electric mixer on low speed for ½ minute, scraping sides of bowl. Beat for 3 minutes at high speed. Stir in as much of the remaining flour as you can with a spoon.
3. Turn dough out onto a lightly floured surface. Knead in enough remaining flour to make a smooth, elastic, moderately soft dough. Shape into a ball. Cover with plastic wrap and dish towel. Let rest 15 minutes.
4. To shape, roll out dough to form a 10x10-inch square. With a floured cutter, cut into 12 doughnuts. On a greased baking sheet (or baking sheet covered with parchment paper or foil), arrange doughnut shapes in a circle. Stretch and elongate rings slightly with your fingers. Cluster holes from rings in the center, cutting additional holes from scraps.
5. Let rise till light (about 1 hour). Bake in a 375° oven for 10 to 12 minutes or till golden. Carefully remove the coffee cake from baking sheet. Brush with melted butter or margarine. Cool.
6. Spoon desired jelly into the centers of the doughnut rings. Drizzle Orange Glaze over cake. Sprinkle centers with toasted almonds. Makes 10 servings.
Orange Glaze: In a mixing bowl, stir together 1¼ cups sifted *powdered sugar*, ⅛ to ¼ teaspoon *almond extract*, 1 teaspoon grated *orange peel*, and 1 tablespoon *orange juice* to make a mixture of drizzling consistency.

Raisin-Lovers' Surprise Loaves

Faith Mikita created this recipe for her son's first entry in the Illinois State Fair.

- 1 cup golden raisins
- 2 tablespoons lemon juice
- 3 to 3½ cups bread flour
- 2 packages active dry yeast
- 2 teaspoons baking powder
- 2 cups buttermilk
- ⅓ cup honey
- 3 tablespoons butter
- 2 teaspoons salt
- 2 cups whole wheat flour
- 2 tablespoons honey
- 2 tablespoons butter, softened
- ½ teaspoon ground cinnamon
   Melted butter
   Walnut Glaze

1. In a small bowl, combine raisins and lemon juice; let stand for 30 minutes. Drain.
2. In a large mixer bowl, combine *2 cups* of the bread flour, yeast, and baking powder.
3. In a small saucepan, heat buttermilk, ⅓ cup honey, 3 tablespoons butter, and salt till very warm (120° to 130°) and butter is almost melted; stir constantly.
4. Stir heated mixture into dry ingredients in mixer bowl. Beat on low speed for 30 seconds. Beat 3 minutes on high. Add whole wheat flour,

*Raisin-Lovers'
Surprise Loaves*

*Sunrise Serenade
Coffee Cake*

drained raisins, and as much of the remaining bread flour as you can with a spoon. Knead in enough flour to make a smooth, elastic, moderately stiff dough (6 to 8 minutes).

5. Cover and let rest for 10 minutes.

6. In a small bowl combine 2 tablespoons honey, 2 tablespoons butter, and cinnamon. Punch down dough. Divide in half. Roll out *half* of the dough into a 12x8-inch rectangle. Brush with *half* of the honey mixture.

7. Starting at an 8-inch side, roll up dough tightly. Seal edges and fold underneath. Place loaf, seam side down, in a greased 8½x4½x2½-inch loaf pan. Repeat with remaining dough

and honey mixture.

8. Cover; let rise till doubled (¾ to 1 hour). Bake in a 350° oven for 40 minutes; cover with foil the last 10 minutes if it gets too brown. Cool. Brush with melted butter. Frost with Walnut Glaze. Makes 2 loaves (32 servings). *Walnut Glaze:* In a bowl beat together 1 cup sifted *powdered sugar*, 2 teaspoons softened *butter*, and 2 to 4 tablespoons *orange juice* till glaze is a spreading consistency. Stir in ½ cup finely chopped *walnuts*.

(Top) Try our state-fair recipes at home and see if you agree with the judges that these recipes are blue-ribbon delicious. (Bottom) Part of the fun of the fair is enjoying the colorful whirling rides on the midway.

17

Judges' Choice German-Chocolate Ice Cream

Former Iowa Governor Robert Ray awarded Joy and David McFarland a blue ribbon for this cool dessert.

> 4 fresh eggs
> 2 cups sugar
> 1 quart light cream
> ¾ cup chocolate syrup
> 1½ teaspoons vanilla
> ⅛ teaspoon salt
> 1 quart whole milk
> ¾ cup chopped pecans
> ¾ cup coconut

1. In a mixer bowl, beat eggs with an electric mixer till light. Add sugar; beat till well combined. Add cream, chocolate syrup, vanilla, and salt; beat well. Stir in milk, pecans, and coconut.
2. Freeze cream mixture in a 4- to 5-quart ice cream freezer according to the manufacturer's directions.
3. Ripen ice cream. Makes 4 quarts (32 servings).

Former Iowa Governor and ice cream fanatic Robert Ray judges ice cream at the Iowa fair.

Chunky Cherry-Cobbler Ice Cream

Joy and David McFarland's 1988 state-fair entry won first place in "hometown pretrials." (In other words, it disappeared faster than other flavors they took to community gatherings.)

> Cobbler Topping
> 6 slightly beaten fresh eggs
> 2 cups sugar
> 1 quart light cream
> 1 4-serving-size package instant
>   vanilla pudding mix
> 1 teaspoon vanilla
>   Dash salt
> 1 21-ounce can cherry-pie filling
> 2 cups whole milk

1. Prepare Cobbler Topping.
2. In a large mixer bowl, beat together the eggs and sugar. Add cream, pudding mix, vanilla, and salt; beat well. Mix in the cherry pie filling.
3. Pour into a 4- to 5-quart ice cream freezer. Add milk. Freeze according to manufacturer's directions.
4. Remove dasher. Add the Cobbler Topping. Stir till well mixed. Ripen ice cream. Makes 4 quarts (32 servings).
Cobbler Topping: In a mixing bowl, stir together 1 cup *rolled oats*, ½ cup *all-purpose flour*, ½ cup packed *brown sugar*, and ½ teaspoon *ground cinnamon*. Stir in ⅓ cup melted *butter* or *margarine*. Spread in a shallow baking pan, and bake in a 350° oven for 20 minutes. Cool.

Chunky Cherry-Cobbler Ice Cream

Ripe 'n' Rich Black Raspberry Ice Cream

Joy McFarland bagged a blue ribbon in the raspberry division of the Iowa State Fair with her refreshing berry ice cream.

6   fresh eggs
2   cups sugar
1   quart light cream
1   4-serving-size package instant vanilla pudding mix
1   tablespoon vanilla
    Dash salt
3   cups whole milk
1½ pints black raspberries or one 12-ounce package frozen black raspberries, thawed

1. In a mixer bowl beat fresh eggs with an electric mixer till light. Add sugar; beat till mixture is well combined. Stir in light cream, instant vanilla pudding mix, vanilla, and salt.
2. Pour into a 4- to 5-quart ice cream freezer. Stir in milk and black raspberries.
3. Freeze in a 4- or 5-quart ice cream freezer according to manufacturer's directions. Ripen. Makes 3½ quarts (28 servings).

Judges' Choice German-Chocolate Ice Cream

Ripening Ice Cream

For the best homemade ice cream, be sure to ripen it to blend the flavors. First, remove the dasher and cover the freezer can with waxed paper. Plug the hole in the freezer lid and place it on the can. Fill the outer freezer bucket with enough ice and rock salt (4 cups ice to 1 cup salt) to cover the can. Ripen for 4 hours.

19

Cherry-Berry Surprise Pie

For her do-your-own-thing entry in the Indiana State Fair, Mary Alice Collins combined cherries and raspberries.

1½ cups frozen cherries
1¼ cups frozen raspberries
     Cherry juice or cranberry juice
       cocktail
     Helen Rushton's Make-Ahead
       Piecrust or Mary Alice Collins'
       Old-Fashioned Lard Piecrust (see
       recipes, opposite)
1¼ cups sugar
  3 tablespoons cornstarch
  1 tablespoon quick-cooking tapioca
  ¼ teaspoon salt
1½ tablespoons butter
1½ teaspoons lemon juice
  ⅛ teaspoon almond flavoring

1. Thaw frozen fruit in a colander over a mixing bowl, reserving juice. Add enough cherry juice or cranberry juice cocktail to equal 1¼ cups.
2. Using 2 balls of piecrust dough, roll each ball into a 12-inch circle. Wrap *one* circle around rolling pin. Unroll onto a 9-inch pie plate. Ease pastry into pie plate (do not stretch pastry). Trim pastry even with pie plate.
3. In a saucepan, combine sugar, cornstarch, tapioca, and salt. Add the reserved juice. Cook and stir till thickened and bubbly. Stir in butter, lemon juice, and almond flavoring. Add the thawed fruit. Cook and stir for 3 to 5 minutes or till thickened.
4. Pour filling into pastry in pie plate. Cut vents into remaining pastry circle. Place circle on top of filling. Trim top crust ½ inch beyond edge of plate. Fold top crust under bottom crust. Seal; flute edges. Bake in a 425° oven for 15 minutes. Reduce oven to 375°; bake for 20 to 30 minutes. Cool. Makes 8 servings.

Pride-o'-the-Fair Chocolate Pie

Super-quick to make and chocolaty— that's Mary Alice Collins' winning pie.

     Helen Rushton's Make-Ahead
       Piecrust or Mary Alice Collins'
       Old-Fashioned Lard Piecrust (see
       recipes, opposite)
  1 cup sugar
  2 tablespoons all-purpose flour
  ⅛ teaspoon salt
  2 cups light cream
  2 1-ounce packages premelted,
       unsweetened chocolate
  3 slightly beaten egg yolks
  2 tablespoons butter
  ½ teaspoon vanilla
     Meringue

1. Prepare and bake 1 piecrust shell. Cool.
2. For filling, in a medium saucepan, combine sugar, flour, and salt. Stir in cream and chocolate. Cook and stir till bubbly. Cook for 2 minutes more.
3. Stir a small amount of the hot mixture (about ½ cup) into yolks. Return all to saucepan. Cook for 2 minutes more; stir constantly. Remove from heat. Stir in butter and vanilla. Pour into shell.
4. Prepare Meringue. Top pie with meringue. Bake in a 350° oven for 12 to 15 minutes or till golden. Store, covered, in the refrigerator. Makes 8 servings.
Meringue: In a mixer bowl, beat 3 *egg whites* and ¼ teaspoon *cream of tartar* till high and frothy. Add 6 tablespoons *sugar*, a tablespoon at a time, beating after each addition till soft peaks form (tips curl). Add ½ teaspoon *vanilla;* beat for 1 minute more. Spread meringue over hot filling, carefully sealing edges. Using the back of a spoon, shape whites into peaks.

Old Faithful Sugar-Cream Pie

Helen Rushton calls her heavenly rich sugar-cream pie "Old Faithful" because it always turns out well.

     Helen Rushton's Make-Ahead
       Piecrust or Mary Alice Collins'
       Old-Fashioned Lard Piecrust (see
       recipes, opposite)
  1 cup sugar
  ¼ cup plus 1½ teaspoons all-purpose
       flour
  1 cup whipping cream
  ½ cup light cream
  ¾ teaspoon vanilla
  ⅛ teaspoon salt
     Ground nutmeg

1. Prepare 1 pie shell*. Do not bake.
2. In a mixer bowl, combine sugar and flour. Add creams, vanilla, and salt. With electric mixer beat for about 6 minutes or till fluffy and thickened. Cover; chill for 1 hour.
3. Pour cream mixture into unbaked shell. Sprinkle with nutmeg. Bake in a 425° oven for 10 minutes. Reduce oven temperature to 375° and bake pie for about 20 minutes more or till a knife inserted near the center comes out clean. Cool. Store, covered, in the refrigerator. Makes 8 servings.
*Note: Because the filling is so rich, this pie is not as deep as a regular pie. To compensate, crimp your pie shell just high enough so the crust is even with the top of the pie plate.

Pride-o'-the-Fair Chocolate Pie

Old Faithful Sugar-Cream Pie

Mary Alice Collins' Old-Fashioned Lard Piecrust

Mary Alice and other pie makers agree: Lard makes a flaky crust.

3 cups all-purpose flour
1 teaspoon salt
1 cup lard
1 tablespoon vinegar
1 beaten egg
1/3 cup cold water

1. In a large bowl combine flour and salt. Cut in lard till mixture resembles a coarse meal.

2. In a small bowl combine vinegar, egg, and cold water. Add egg mixture, a tablespoon at a time, to flour mixture. Toss to form a soft dough. Divide dough into thirds. Shape each third into a ball. Wrap each ball in waxed paper. Chill for 3 to 24 hours.

3. Roll out each third of the pastry to form a 12-inch circle. Ease pastry into a 9-inch pie plate. Trim to 1/2 inch beyond edge of plate. Flute edge. Prick bottom and sides with fork or line with a double thickness of heavy-duty foil.

4. For a baked shell, bake in a 425° oven for 10 minutes. Reduce oven to 375° and bake for 20 minutes more. Makes 3 single piecrusts.

Helen Rushton's Make-Ahead Piecrust

When baking dozens of pies for the fair, Helen rolls and cuts her crusts several days before baking. Then, she stores them in the freezer to "set" the dough.

3 cups all-purpose flour
1 teaspoon salt
1 cup plus 1 tablespoon butter-flavored shortening
1/3 cup cold water
1 tablespoon vinegar
1 beaten egg

1. In a large bowl combine the flour and salt. Cut in the shortening till mixture resembles cornmeal.

2. In a small bowl combine water, vinegar, and egg. Add egg mixture, a tablespoon at a time, to flour mixture, tossing to form a soft dough. Divide dough into thirds. Shape each portion into a ball. Wrap each ball in waxed paper. Cover; chill for 3 to 24 hours*.

3. Roll out each portion into a 12-inch circle. Ease into a 9-inch pie plate. Trim to 1/2 inch beyond edge of plate. Flute edge.

4. For a baked pie shell, line pastry with double thickness of heavy-duty foil. Bake in a 425° oven 10 minutes. Reduce oven to 375°. Bake 20 minutes or till golden. Makes 3 single crusts.
*Note: To roll out the piecrust immediately, use a well-floured surface.

21

HARVEST TIME IN
Cranberry Country

Where do they all come from?" Bette Goldsworthy marvels, as she frantically fills orders for the throng packed into the bakery tent at Eagle River, Wisconsin's, annual Cranberry Fest. It's early afternoon on the festival's opening day, and already the hungry crowd has downed 80 dozen cranberry fritters and uncounted muffins, cookies, and slabs of pie. Steaming cups of hot spiced cranberry punch also are among the big hits on this sunny but blustery autumn Saturday.

"This weather is good," Bette says, brushing her silver hair back from her forehead. "We need the cold to make the berries turn red."

With crisp October breezes sending fishing boats bouncing toward the docks along northern Wisconsin's endless chain of lakes, and fall's brilliant foliage fluttering to the forest floor, it's time for another crimson harvest in cranberry country.

FOOD-LOVERS' FESTIVAL

That's reason to celebrate in a state that grows more than one-third of the nation's cranberries (Wisconsin and Massachusetts always are the top producers). From across the Midwest, folks flock to the Eagle River celebration, held the first weekend in October in this resorty north-woods hamlet's riverside park. Visitors tour bogs where the cranberries grow, dance to the music of the Wisconsin River Boys, sip cranberry wine, shop at the flea market, and "oooh" and "aah" over the cook-off entries.

But mostly festival-goers eat. A constantly replenished stream of treats from Eagle River kitchens buries the bakery tent's sawhorse tables. All the baked goods are chock-full of berries from the Goldsworthy family's Thunder Lake, One Stone, and Tomahawk marshes (each with several bogs). Bette's husband Charlie oversees the bogs, with help from sons Mark and Tim.

continued

(Left) Beautifully ripe cranberries float on the bogs. (Right) The Goldsworthys—Bette and Charlie.

Cranberry Primer

Don't just save cranberries for Thanksgiving. With this roundup of cranberry dos and don'ts, you can enjoy them anytime in breads, main dishes, salads, and desserts.

To shop for fresh cranberries, look for plump, unblemished berries with a uniform red color. (The lightness or darkness of the color doesn't affect the quality.) Be sure to discard soft or bruised berries.

To store fresh bagged cranberries, refrigerate them for up to four weeks. Or, overwrap the bag of cranberries with freezer wrap and freeze it for up to nine months. You won't have to thaw the berries to use them.

Chopping cranberries by hand can be a real chore. To speed up the job, chop them, a few cups at a time, in your food processor. You should get about 3 cups of chopped berries from a 12-ounce package.

After four decades of growth, the Goldsworthy operation, founded by Charlie's father Vernon, is the major cranberry producer in the area.

A MARSHY LAND'S BOUNTY

Cranberries thrive in the marshy lowlands of northern and central Wisconsin. Domestic cranberries begin as cuttings stamped into shallow, man-made bogs. After four or five years, the ankle-high evergreens are ready to produce fruit for a century.

The Goldsworthy bogs burst into bloom around July 4th. Charlie rents nearly 100 hives of bees to pollinate his plants. By late summer, the berries are plump and tart, awaiting autumn's chill.

THE SCARLET FLOOD

While Eagle River celebrates, Charlie, Mark, and Tim race to harvest 240 acres of berries before winter sets in.

Gates opened on nearby ponds release a knee-deep flood into bogs where berries grow. The fruit floats to the surface as it's gently dislodged by a mechanical beater. Floating booms corral the berries into a solid sea of red. Conveyors load the berries onto trucks destined for the processing plant, where the fruit is bagged or transformed into juice, sauce, jam, jelly—even vinegar.

As they harvest, Charlie and the boys eat handfuls of the mouth-puckering fruit straight from the bogs. "I don't know how they do it," says Bette, who prefers her berries tucked into sweet baked treats.

For details about this year's festival, contact: Eagle River Information Bureau, Box 218, Eagle River, WI 54521 (715/479-8575).

Gently dislodged by a mechanical beater,
the ripe berries float to the surface.

(Top and bottom) Visitors to the Cranberry Fest enjoy all the scrumptious delicacies at the cook-off tent.

Van's Cranberry Fritters

"Cranberry fritters are popular year-round," says George Van Beynen III, who brings these treats to the Cranberry Fest from nearby Woodruff, Wisconsin (see recipe photo, page 28).

4½ to 5 cups all-purpose flour
2 packages active dry yeast
1½ teaspoons baking powder
⅔ cup sugar
½ cup shortening
¼ cup nonfat dry milk powder
1½ teaspoons salt
3 eggs
1 teaspoon vanilla
2 cups chopped, fresh cranberries
Shortening or cooking oil for deep-fat frying
Doughnut Glaze

1. In a mixer bowl, combine *1½ cups* of the flour, the yeast, and the baking powder. In a saucepan, heat the sugar, ½ cup shortening, dry milk powder, salt, and ⅔ cup *water* just till warm (120° to 130°) and shortening is almost melted, stirring constantly.

2. Add to flour mixture; add eggs and vanilla. Beat with an electric mixer on low speed for 30 seconds, scraping sides of bowl constantly. Beat on high speed for 3 minutes. Using a spoon, stir in cranberries and as much of the remaining flour as you can.

3. Turn out onto a lightly floured surface. Knead in enough of the remaining flour to make a moderately soft dough that's smooth (except for the cranberries) and elastic (3 to 5 minutes total). Shape into a ball. Place in a lightly greased bowl; turn once to grease surface. Cover and let rise in a warm place till doubled (1½ hours).

4. Punch dough down. Divide in half. Cover and let rest for 10 minutes. Roll out each half to a ½-inch-thick rectangle, about 12x9 inches. Cut each half into twelve 3x3-inch squares.

5. Meanwhile, heat shortening or oil to 350°. Fry 2 or 3 fritters at a time about 3 minutes or till golden, turning once. Drain. Spoon Doughnut Glaze over fritters while warm. Makes 24.

Doughnut Glaze: In a saucepan, combine ½ cup *water,* ¼ cup *sugar,* and 2 tablespoons *light corn syrup.* Cook and stir till bubbly. Add 2¾ cups *powdered sugar* and ½ teaspoon *vanilla;* stir till smooth. Cool slightly. Makes 2⅔ cups.

Cranberry Candy-Bar Cookies

Irene Johnson, one of the winningest cook-off contestants ever, created these gooey bar cookies—and took home a first prize (see photo, page 29).

1   14-ounce package vanilla caramels
⅓   cup light cream
1   package (2-layer-size) German
       chocolate cake mix
⅓   cup light cream
¼   cup melted butter
1   teaspoon vanilla
1   16-ounce can whole cranberry sauce
½   cup chopped pecans

1. In a heavy 1½-quart saucepan, melt unwrapped caramels in ⅓ cup cream over low heat, stirring occasionally. When caramels are melted, stir till smooth. Set aside.

2. Meanwhile, in a large mixer bowl, combine German chocolate cake mix, ⅓ cup light cream, melted butter, and vanilla. Beat with an electric mixer till smooth. Pat *half of the mixture* in the bottom of a greased 13x9x2-inch baking pan. Bake in a 350° oven for 10 minutes; remove from oven.

3. Spread with warm caramel mixture. Stir cranberry sauce; spoon over caramel layer. Dot remaining cake mixture over cranberry layer. Sprinkle with the chopped pecans. Bake in the 350° oven for 30 minutes. Cool in pan. To serve, cut into bars. You may wish to serve with forks. Makes about 20 cookies.

To Use Your Microwave Oven: Melt caramels by unwrapping and placing them in a 4-cup microwave-safe measure with ⅓ cup light cream. Micro-cook, uncovered, on 100% power (high), stirring every minute for 2½ to 3½ minutes, or till caramels are soft enough to stir smooth. Some pieces won't look melted.

Another favorite at the Eagle River celebration is the pitchers and pitchers of hot cranberry punch.

Winner's-Circle Salad

Judging Contest Entries

When Otto Schmidt samples cookies, pies, salads, or anything else featuring cranberries, he expects a tart little nip back from the berries. "If it's going to be cranberry, then cranberry should be the predominant  *flavor," advises the retired baker, who often judges the cook-off at Eagle River's Cranberry Fest. Breads and desserts dominate the competition. But in the miscellaneous category, Otto nibbles everything from layered salads to main-course casseroles. Whatever the entry, "Don't over-power the cranberries," Otto cautions contestants.*

Van's Cranberry Fritters

Cranberry-Apple-Nut Pie

Cranberry Candy-Bar Cookies

*Blue-Ribbon
Cranberry Chicken*

Judge Rene Ayvazzadeh (above)

expects cook-off entries to look as good

as they taste. But, "Let the berry

taste prevail," adds contest judge

Otto Schmidt.

Winner's-Circle Salad

Gayle Johnson-Moravec, who keeps pace with her mother Irene when it comes to cranberry cook-off honors, created this gala two-tone salad (see photo, page 28).

- ⅓ cup sugar
- 1 envelope unflavored gelatin
- ½ cup cranberry juice cocktail
- ¾ cup chopped fresh cranberries
- ¾ cup ginger ale
- ⅓ cup cranberry liqueur
- 2 3-ounce packages pineapple/orange-flavored gelatin
- 1½ cups water
- 1 pint pineapple or orange sherbet, cut up
- 1 8-ounce carton dairy sour cream
- ¾ cup finely chopped walnuts
- ½ cup finely chopped, fresh cranberries Greens (optional) Frosted Cranberries (optional)

1. In a medium saucepan, stir together the sugar and unflavored gelatin. Add the cranberry juice cocktail; heat and stir till gelatin is completely dissolved. Stir in ¾ cup chopped cranberries, ginger ale, and cranberry liqueur. Turn into a 6- to 7-cup mold (cranberries will float). Cover and chill till almost set, about 60 minutes.

2. In a saucepan, stir together the pineapple/orange gelatin and water; stir over medium heat till gelatin is completely dissolved. Add sherbet; stir till melted and blended. Gradually blend in sour cream; whisk till smooth. Cover; chill till partially set. Stir in nuts and ½ cup chopped cranberries.

3. Spoon sherbet mixture over almost-set first layer in mold. Cover and chill till mixture is set.

4. To serve, line a serving plate with greens, if desired. Unmold salad onto greens. Trim salad with Frosted Cranberries, if desired. Serves 12.

Frosted Cranberries: Dip *cranberries* in *light corn syrup;* coat with *sugar.*

Cranberry-Apple-Nut Pie

This delicious marriage of fall fruits won Nan Pophal of Eagle River a prize in the Cranberry Fest cook-off (see photo, page 29).

- 2 cups fresh cranberries, chopped
- 2 cups chopped, peeled apple
- 1 to 1½ cups sugar
- ½ cup chopped nuts
- 2 tablespoons quick-cooking tapioca
- ¼ teaspoon ground cinnamon Pastry for 9-inch, double-crust pie Milk (optional) Sugar (optional)

1. In a large mixing bowl, combine cranberries, apple, 1 to 1½ cups sugar, nuts, tapioca, and cinnamon. Let stand for 20 minutes.

2. Turn cranberry mixture into a 9-inch, pastry-lined pie plate. Adjust top crust; seal and flute edges. For a fancy finish, flute edge loosely. Using a fork, press fork prints in each rounded flute. Cut vents in top crust. Brush top crust with milk and sprinkle with additional sugar, if desired. Cover edge of pie with foil to prevent overbrowning.

3. Bake in a 375° oven for 25 minutes; remove foil. Bake for 20 to 30 minutes more or till golden. Makes 8 servings.

Blue-Ribbon Cranberry Chicken

This first-prize entry in the contest's "miscellaneous" category is a dinner winner from Eagle River's Catherine Snedden. It's easy to make, colorful, and pleasantly piquant (see photo, pages 28 and 29).

1 16-ounce can whole cranberry sauce
1 8-ounce bottle reduced-calorie Russian salad dressing with honey (about 1 cup) or regular Russian salad dressing
1 envelope regular onion-soup mix
1 2½- to 3-pound broiler-fryer chicken, cut up
  Hot cooked rice (optional)
  Fresh rosemary (optional)

1. In a bowl, combine cranberry sauce, salad dressing, and soup mix. Rinse chicken; pat dry with paper towels. Remove and discard skin, if desired. Arrange pieces in one layer in a 13x9x2-inch baking dish. Pour cranberry mixture over chicken pieces. Cover and chill the chicken mixture in the refrigerator for several hours or overnight.
2. Bake the chicken mixture, uncovered, in a 300° oven about 1½ hours or till the chicken is done, stirring glaze and spooning over chicken once or twice. Serve the chicken and glaze on a platter with hot, cooked rice, if desired. Garnish the chicken with fresh rosemary, if desired. Makes 4 servings.

Perennial cook-off winners Irene Johnson and daughter Gayle Johnson-Moravec.

A HARVEST OF GOOD EATING AND GREAT FUN
Sweet Corn

Hands down, the Heartland grows more sweet corn than anywhere else. Wisconsin and Minnesota lead the way (more than 1.1 millon tons annually, combined). But Illinois ranks No. 1 in corny festivals. Every year, thousands flock to the town of Hoopeston to feast on buttery ears. Join the sweet-corn harvest celebration and learn new ways to prepare the Midwest's choice bumper crop.

COME CELEBRATE

"Hot corn! Hot corn!" echoes the cry as crowds push toward mounds of sunshine-colored ears slathered in butter. Ready with every kind of container—from cardboard boxes and backpacks to oven roasters and picnic coolers—thousands of munchers gather for the National Sweet Corn Festival in the farming and canning community of Hoopeston, Illinois, 100 miles south of Chicago.

During a year's celebration, corn-crazy throngs devour or carry home 45 tons of ears, cooked to perfection with the help of an old-fashioned steam engine. As one butter-drenched bystander wisecracked, "It's complete 'cornage.'"

Along with baseball games and swimming holes, sweet corn is synonymous with summer in the Midwest. As tasseling stalks stretch straight and tall, we anxiously check for drying silks. Then, with mouth-watering smiles, we greet golden platters of corn on the cob.

33

Townspeople and visitors alike come early to stake out a good curbside seat to watch the parade.

Twelve thousand acres of sweet corn surround Hoopeston (population: 6,400). That's enough to keep two shifts at the Stokely USA corn-canning plant humming all summer long.

The approaching end of the sweet-corn season signals the start of Hoopeston's festival. Launched in 1938, the festival attracts an estimated 60,000-plus each year.

Free corn on the cob highlights the last three days of the celebration. Naturally, there's a big corn-eating competition. The winner in the adult division usually chomps more than five ears in three minutes.

CORNY COMPETITIONS

But free corn isn't the only festival attraction. McFerren Park teems with carnival rides, kids' games, concerts, demolition derbies, a national beauty pageant, classic-car exhibit, flea market, fishing derby, and talent and art show.

The competition is formidable. Over at the horseshoe pits, for example, contestants come from 100 miles away every year, says Willard Bruen, a 40-year veteran pitcher. Competitors at the top rung of the six-class ladder throw ringers 65 to 75 percent of the time. (Pitch a ringer with at least one of every five throws and you can qualify for the lowest level of competition.)

PARADES, PAGEANTS

Hoopeston Jaycees, who organize the event, donate all the proceeds to local charities. Everyone in town contributes something. That includes Stokely USA, which donates all the free sweet corn.

continued on page 36

A Corny Calendar

There's no better way to spend a summer day than at a Midwest sweet-corn fest. Here's a guide to the revelry you'll find in store at assorted sweet-corn festivals throughout the Heartland.

July
Illinois:
 Corn Boil—Pavilion Park, Sugar Grove (800/447-4369).

Iowa:
 Sweet Corn Day—downtown Elkader (319/245-2372).

August
Illinois:
 Corn Festival—downtown Mendota (815/539-6507).

 Corn Festival—downtown Normal (309/452-1360).

 Annual Corn Fest—Seven Acres Antique Village, Union (815/923-2214).

 Corn Festival—downtown DeKalb (815/756-6306).

 National Corn Festival—Hoopeston (217/283-7873).

Iowa:
 Sweet Corn Day—town square, Oskaloosa (515/673-7401).

 Sweet Corn Festival—town square, Adel (515/993-5265).

 St. Jude's Sweet Corn Festival—St. Jude's Church, Cedar Rapids (319/390-3520).

Ohio:
 Corn Festival—downtown North Ridgeville (216/327-9019).

 Sweet Corn Festival—Millersport (614/467-2333).

Wisconsin:
 Corn Roast—Scandinavia (715/445-3653).

 Corn Fest—Angell Park, Sun Prairie (608/837-4547).

September
Illinois:
 Corn Carnival—town square, Milton (217/285-2971).

 Corn and Bean Festival—downtown Oakland (217/346-2341).

 The Corn Festival—downtown Morris (815/942-0113).

Indiana:
 Sullivan County Jaycees Corn Festival—town square, Sullivan (812/268-4836).

Ohio:
 Clinton County Corn Festival—fairgrounds, Wilmington (513/382-4684).

South Dakota:
 Corn Palace Festival—Mitchell (605/996-5567).

Bushel after bushel of prime quality corn finds its way from the field to the cannery or the local festival during the sweet corn season.

The crowning glory of the festival is the National Sweetheart Pageant, which a local Miss Sweet Corn competition spawned. Five past National Sweethearts have been named Miss America (most recently Carolyn Sapp, Miss America 1991), proving that Hoopeston judges know how to pick more than sweet corn.

SWEET, STEAMING CORN

During all the goings-on, the ears keep bubbling. How do you cook 45 tons of sweet corn to feed the crowds? "First," says Steve Eyrich, who works for a Hoopeston firm that manufactures canning equipment, "you get an old-fashioned steam engine and replumb it."

The massive iron monster, belching black coal smoke amid rising clouds of shimmering steam, circulates boiling water through a series of shiny cattle troughs. Jaycees volunteers dunk basketfuls of fresh sweet corn—which an antique shucking machine husks—into the steamy bath. After that, the volunteers dump the corn into huge pans and hand-butter the ears using giant brushes.

Corn-loving throngs that gather watch each step, as if the ears were crisp $20 bills. Finally comes the shout everyone is waiting to hear: "Hot corn! Hot corn!" After that, it's everyone for himself.

The festival hits its stride on Saturday, when a big parade winds through town to McFerren Park. Parade enthusiasts line the curbs. As the procession sweeps past the town's two canneries and a can-making plant, Stokely employees and others unfortunate enough to have to work their regular jobs during the busy sweet-corn harvest season lean from open windows to cheer.

For more information about the Hoopeston celebration, contact: National Sweet Corn Festival, Hoopeston Chamber of Commerce, Box 346, Hoopeston, IL 60942 (217/283-7873).

Puffy Skillet Corn Fritters

Puffy Skillet Corn Fritters

Corn flavors this double-duty side dish: It's a vegetable and a bread.

1 tablespoon butter
2 cups fresh corn kernels
¼ cup chopped green pepper
¼ cup chopped onion
¼ cup all-purpose flour
½ teaspoon baking powder
½ teaspoon salt
¼ teaspoon pepper
2 beaten eggs
2 tablespoons milk
2 dashes bottled hot pepper sauce
2 to 3 tablespoons cooking oil

1. In a medium saucepan, melt butter. Add corn, green pepper, and onion. Cook, covered, for 8 minutes, stirring occasionally. Cool slightly.
2. In a mixing bowl combine flour, baking powder, salt, and pepper. Add eggs, milk, and hot pepper sauce. Mix well. Stir in slightly cooled vegetable mixture.
3. In a large skillet, heat cooking oil over medium heat. Drop corn mixture by heaping tablespoonfuls, 4 or 5 at a time, into hot oil. Flatten slightly with the back of a spoon. Cook about 4 minutes or till brown, turning once. (If fritters brown too quickly, reduce heat.) Drain on paper towels. Serve warm with meat or poultry. Makes twelve 3½-inch fritters (6 servings).

Bountiful Corn Stir-Fry

Turn this trio of the season's "bests" into a tasty side dish straight from your skillet or wok.

½ teaspoon cornstarch
½ teaspoon sugar
½ teaspoon salt
¼ teaspoon pepper
¼ cup chicken or beef broth
3 tablespoons cooking oil
2 cloves garlic, minced
¼ cup bias-sliced green onion
2 cups fresh corn kernels
1 cup julienne-cut zucchini
1 cup sliced fresh mushrooms

1. In a small bowl, combine cornstarch, sugar, salt, and pepper. Stir in chicken or beef broth. Set mixture aside.
2. In a 12-inch skillet or wok, heat cooking oil over high heat. Add garlic and green onion; stir-fry for 30 seconds.
3. Add corn, zucchini, and mushrooms; stir-fry for 2 minutes. Add broth mixture to skillet. Cook and stir till slightly thickened and bubbly. Cook and stir for 1 minute more. Makes 4 to 6 servings.

Bountiful Corn Stir-Fry

Spicy Corn-Stuffed Tomato Salad

When summer gets steamy, team up these two abundant Midwest vegetables in a cool salad.

---

      6 small, ripe tomatoes
    ½ cup creamy buttermilk salad dressing
      2 tablespoons snipped parsley
    ¼ teaspoon pepper
      Dash ground red pepper
      2 cups cooked fresh corn kernels
    ½ cup shredded Monterey Jack cheese
    ¼ cup chopped green pepper
    ¼ cup chopped cucumber
    ¼ cup chopped onion
      Lettuce leaves

1. Place tomatoes, stem end down, on a cutting surface. Cut each into 4 to 6 wedges, cutting to, but not through, stem end. Spread wedges apart slightly; sprinkle with *salt.* Cover; chill.
2. In a small mixing bowl, combine buttermilk salad dressing, parsley, pepper, and red pepper.
3. In another bowl, combine corn, cheese, green pepper, cucumber, and onion. Add dressing mixture; toss gently to coat. Cover and chill.
4. To serve, arrange tomatoes atop lettuce leaves on individual plates. Fill the tomatoes with corn mixture. Makes 6 servings.

Grilled Ham and Corn Kabobs

Fresh apricots make a surprise appearance in this skewered main dish—perfect for a barbecue.

---

      2 ears of fresh corn
      1 5½-ounce can (⅔ cup) apricot
          nectar
      2 tablespoons honey
      1 tablespoon lemon juice
      2 teaspoons prepared mustard
    1½ pounds fully cooked ham, cut into
          1-inch pieces
      2 medium green peppers, cut into
          1½-inch pieces
      1 pound fresh apricots, halved or
          quartered and pitted

1. Cut ears of corn into 1½-inch-long pieces. Blanch the corn in boiling water for 9 minutes. (Begin timing immediately after adding the corn to the boiling water.) Drain.
2. In a small saucepan, combine the apricot nectar, honey, lemon juice, and mustard. Bring to boiling. Reduce heat; boil gently for 10 to 15 minutes or till slightly thickened.
3. Meanwhile, on 6 long skewers, thread ham, green pepper pieces, apricot halves or quarters, and corn.
4. Grill over *medium-hot* coals for 8 to 12 minutes or till vegetables are tender, turning often. Brush occasionally with honey mixture during grilling. Makes 6 servings.

Spicy Corn-Stuffed Tomato Salad

Grilled Ham and Corn Kabobs

Corny Corn Bread

Corn-Tomato Relish

Corn-Tomato Relish

Can or freeze this not-too-sweet, not-too-tart relish.

6 to 8 ears of fresh corn
½ cup boiling water
2 cups peeled, seeded, and chopped tomatoes (4 or 5 medium)
1¼ cups peeled, seeded, and chopped cucumber (about 1 medium)
¾ cup seeded and chopped green pepper (about 1 medium)
¾ cup chopped onion
½ cup chopped celery
1 cup cider vinegar
¾ cup sugar
1 tablespoon salt
1 tablespoon dry mustard
1 teaspoon celery seed
½ teaspoon ground turmeric

1. Cut enough corn from the cobs to measure 4 cups. In an 8- to 10-quart kettle or Dutch oven cook corn, covered, in the ½ cup boiling water about 4 minutes or till nearly tender.
2. Add remaining ingredients to the corn. Bring to boiling. Cook, uncovered, for 10 minutes.
3. Meanwhile, set a boiling-water canner with rack on the range. Add 4 to 5 inches of water. Cover and heat on high heat. Heat additional water.
4. Pack hot relish into hot, clean, ½- or 1-pint jars, leaving ½-inch headspace. Wipe jar rims; adjust lids. Place on rack of canner. Fill canner with boiling water so water is 2 inches above jar tops.
5. Replace cover; heat water to a brisk, rolling boil. Begin timing. Process for 15 minutes, keeping water boiling gently and adding boiling water if level drops. Remove jars. Cool completely; check seals. Makes 7 half-pints or 3½ pints.
To freeze relish: Cool the relish. Spoon relish into freezer containers. Seal, label, and freeze.

Corny Corn Bread

Double your pleasure with this quintessential Midwest treat from your oven. It melds two wholesome flavors: corn and bacon.

1 cup all-purpose flour
1 cup yellow cornmeal
¼ cup sugar
4 teaspoons baking powder
¾ teaspoon salt
2 slightly beaten eggs
1 cup milk
¼ cup cooking oil or shortening, melted
1 cup fresh corn kernels
4 slices bacon, crisp-cooked, drained, and crumbled

1. In a mixing bowl, combine flour, cornmeal, sugar, baking powder, and salt. Add eggs, milk, and cooking oil or melted shortening. Beat till smooth. Stir in corn and crumbled bacon. Turn into a greased 9x9x2-inch baking pan.
2. Bake the corn bread in a 425° oven for 20 to 25 minutes or till golden brown. Makes 8 or 9 servings.

The Midwest can be justly proud to be known as the "breadbasket of the nation." Not only do sun-soaked fields of corn, wheat, and oats decorate the landscape, but so do fruit-laden orchards, wild-rice-rich wetlands, and majestic

Farms

stands of nut trees. On the next few pages, we'll take you on a tour of the countryside in Wisconsin, Michigan, Iowa, Missouri, North Dakota, and Minnesota. You'll savor just-picked apples and learn how to use them in everything from apple butter to apple pie. We'll show you the cream of the crop when it comes to berry farms. There, you can get your fill of plump, juicy blueberries and strawberries. Then, you can discover the rich nutty flavor of fresh sunflower kernels, aromatic black walnuts, hand-harvested wild rice, and earthy morel mushrooms. Finally, join us for greens hunting in the Ozarks. Whatever your taste, you're sure to find something you'll like at one of these stops.

GREAT TIMES, GOOD EATING
At the Old Apple Orchard

Carl Rentschler and his grand-children gather to harvest the apples from their rented family tree.

I t's easy to spot the regulars at Tree-Mendus Fruit, a Michigan you-pick farm. Like Carl Rentschler and his grandchildren (left), they head straight for the registration counter to sign up to pick fruit. First-timers stop short at the bins out front, marveling: "I never knew there were so many kinds of apples!"

If Herb Teichman, owner of the 650-acre Tree-Mendus farm near Eau Claire, is within earshot, he's quick to softly explain, "We grow 200 apple varieties here." Herb points to a list on the wall: Pumpkin Sweet, Claygate Pearmain, Dolgo Crab, Ellison's Orange, Hoople's Antique Gold, Limbertwig. Each name is more exotic than the last; each suggests a story. And Herb knows them all.

"An Iowa farmer named Jesse Hiatt," Herb Teichman begins a favorite tale, "had a pesky wild tree growing along his fence. He cut it down—twice. But it kept coming back, so he let it grow.

"The apples that tree produced were odd—with five bumps on the bottom. But these were the best apples Jesse ever tasted, so he named them Hawkeye and entered them in a Missouri fruit show.

"When Mr. Stark, president of the Stark Nursery Company, sampled the fruit, he declared, 'This is delicious,' and it's been called the Delicious apple ever since."

A FAMILY OF APPLE PROS

Herb's family has been in the apple business since his father bought the original 160-acre Tree-Mendus farm more than 60 years ago. Now, Herb's son, Bill, is a partner. Daughter Cindy and her husband work at the farm, and daughter Lynne helps out at the market on busy summer weekends, when she isn't working as a horticultural research technician at Michigan State University. Herb's wife, Liz, is in charge of the books.

Pick-your-own farms are common in Michigan's fruit belt, a narrow strip along the eastern shore of Lake Michigan. Orchards stretch as far as you can see. During the harvest season, late June to mid-October, folks drive from Chicago, South Bend, Detroit, and points beyond to pick their share of fruit.

"This trip is something that families do together," says Herb. "Harvesting their fruit is an annual event. Youngsters remember it, and then when they grow up, they come back and bring along their kids."

A special option at Tree-Mendus farm is renting a family tree. For an annual fee, you can pick and take home all the apples that grow on that tree.

THE RENTSCHLER REUNION

One cool weekend every October, three generations of Rentschlers gather at their trees to pick, picnic, and reminisce. Carl, the family patriarch, still keeps the newspaper clipping from more than a dozen years ago in which he learned about the rental trees. That first year, only Carl; his late wife, Grace; and daughter Susan and her husband Allan made the four-hour drive to Tree-Mendus from Grosse Point, Michigan.

"We searched awhile among all the trees until we saw the one tied with the bright yellow ribbon that had our name on it," Carl smiles. "But we had so much fun—the following year, we brought the rest of the family."

Today, the Rentschlers rent three apple trees and their clan fills several cars. There's Carl; sons David and Donald and their wives; Susan and her husband; and all the grandchildren: Brian, Amy, Douglas, Karen, Kristin, Christopher, Mindy, Peter, and Tommy.

Not everyone makes it every year, but most do. Often, friends of the family come along, too. The trip is a tradition, David Rentschler explains. "We're all committed to continuing it, even after Dad is gone."

The family picks their apples quickly. "We've had years of experience," Susan offers. They eat lots of apples while they're at it and advise each other on technique: "Try to keep the stems on: That's it, just lift and twist . . . ."

When all the apples are picked, bagged, and divided, the kids play, and the adults take pictures. But mostly they visit, as families tend to do.

BUSTLING PICKERS' HAVEN

Herb Teichman tries to make his visitors' days in the country memorable—fruitful, you might say. You can hike trails in the Tree-Mendus wilderness sanctuary, picnic, and turn kids loose at the playgrounds. On the weekends, a wagon that's drawn by a Belgian horse team hauls pickers to the orchards.

There's a guided tour of all the farm's technical operations. You see the experimental orchards, including one where apple trees grow on trellises, and learn that some fruit trees need to be rotated about once a decade, instead of every year like most grains.

"How many trees do you have here at the farm?" one Tree-Mendus visitor calls from the back of the wagon.

"Over 40,000," Herb proudly responds.

"It's quite a science, isn't it?" another visitor comments. Herb just smiles.

The Tree-Mendus Fruit market is almost always buzzing. Besides selling pre-picked fruit (usually at the same price as self-picked), the store stocks fruit cookbooks, including one that features recipes of Herb's mother. Home-canned fruits and jellies, cider, kitchen utensils, and souvenirs complete the market's inventory.

In the fall, apple butter bubbles in a huge copper pot outside the market. Children line up to take turns stirring. But you won't get the

continued

Wearing his trademark cap, Herb Teichman, who's an apple man to the core, orchestrates his fruit market like a classroom.

43

Teichman apple-butter recipe, no matter who you ask or how hard you try.

Then, there's the apple sampling. First, you can nibble a Holiday apple slice, followed by a Red Rome. "The Holiday is a sweet-tart apple," Herb volunteers. "Its flavor explodes in your mouth."

"Oh, it does," exclaims one apple muncher. "It's good!"

A LABOR OF LOVE

In his Museum Orchard, Herb grows more than 200 antique varieties of apples—trees that might have been familiar to early colonists, but now largely have disappeared.

Herb planted the antique orchard in 1976, as a bicentennial project. Though he confesses he didn't do well in history in school ("I couldn't keep all the battles straight"), Herb figured he could relate history to something he understood—apples. "My father," Herb smiles, "loved history. He was a student of old apple varieties and always wanted to preserve them, but never got to. This orchard is for him."

SIMPLE BEGINNINGS

When William, Herb's father, went to work on a fruit farm after World War I, he took a truckload of apples to Fort Wayne, Indiana, where he sold them near the railroad station. One train engineer liked some of those apples so much that he sent his daughter back for more. His daughter was Herb's mother, Leona—or Mimi, as she's more often called.

Because their romance sparked over a basket of Jonathans, William's first planting was 15 acres of Jonathans. "Planting so many acres

in one variety was unheard of then," Mimi recalls.

That first year on the farm was tough. William lived in a tent while the house was being built. The fireplace mantel, assembled from stones on the farm, was Mimi's wedding present. Draft horses hauled all the stones, except one, up the hill. That last stone—too heavy for the horses—lay near the house for 41 years before it was moved to mark William's grave.

Mimi still lives in the hilltop house, with its commanding view of a sea of trees and the sunset. As afternoon shadows lengthen, you start to appreciate Herb's vision: to make Tree-Mendus a farm his family is proud of and a farm families like the Rentschlers come back to year after year.

PICKING PARTICULARS

Tree-Mendus Fruit stays open daily, except Tuesdays, from late June through Labor Day. After Labor Day until mid-October, the farm is open Fridays through Mondays. Tours are scheduled other times by appointment.

The apple harvest lasts from late July through early October. In addition to apples, Tree-Mendus Fruit grows cherries, apricots, plums, peaches, nectarines, and pears. It's a good idea to call the Tree-Mendus Ripe 'N' Ready Reports (616/782-7101) before visiting.

The farm is located in south-western Michigan, 1½ miles off State-140, which is accessible from I-80, I-90, I-94, or I-96. Call 616/782-7101 to get specific directions.

For other you-pick apple farms located around the Midwest, see boxes, left and opposite.

The Carl Rentschler clan, all apple-picking pros, lend each other a hand. "That's just the kind of family we are," says Carl.

APPLE HARVEST OUTINGS
(continued from opposite page)
KANSAS

Kansas Fresh Produce Directory, Board of Agriculture, Marketing, 901 S. Kansas Ave., Topeka, KS 66612-1282 (913/296-3736).

MICHIGAN

Farm Market and U-Pick Directory, Michigan Department of Agriculture, Marketing Division, P.O. Box 30017, Lansing, MI 48909 (517/373-1058).

MINNESOTA

Farmer to Consumer Directory, Minnesota Office of Tourism, 375 Jackson St., 250 Skyway, St. Paul, MN 55101 (296-5029 in the Twin Cities, 800/657-3700 elsewhere).

MISSOURI

Retail Apple Crop Listing, Market Development Division, Missouri Department of Agriculture, Box 630, Jefferson City, MO 65102 (314/751-3394).

NORTH DAKOTA

North Dakota Products and Services Directory, North Dakota Department of Agriculture, State Capitol, 600 E. Boulevard Ave., Bismarck, ND 58505 (701/224-2231).

OHIO

The Ohio Apple Marketing Program, Box 479, Columbus, OH 43216 (614/249-2424). Ask this agency to provide the names of orchards.

WISCONSIN

Fresh Apples and Apple Products, Wisconsin Department of Agriculture, Marketing Division, 801 W. Badger Rd., Box 8911, Madison, WI 53708-8911 (608/266-1531).

Grow up on a fruit farm, as Cindy Teichman DeValk did, and you're bound to peel lots of apples.

Bill Teichman whips up a huge pot of apple butter, much to the delight of visitors.

Brandied Apple Roll-Ups

This Teichman family favorite is even tastier topped with whipped cream that's spiced with ground cinnamon!

- ¼ cup sugar
- 1 tablespoon cornstarch
  Chunky Applesauce
- ¼ cup brandy
- 24 Mini Crepes (see recipe, page 48)
- 1 tablespoon sugar
- ¼ teaspoon ground cinnamon

1. For filling, in a small saucepan, combine the ¼ cup sugar and cornstarch. Stir in Chunky Applesauce and brandy. Cook and stir over medium heat till mixture is thickened and bubbly. Remove from heat.
2. On each Mini Crepe, spoon a scant *1 tablespoon* of the filling along 1 edge of the unbrowned side. Roll up tightly. Place, seam side down, in a greased shallow baking pan. Bake, uncovered, in a 350° oven about 10 minutes or till heated through.
3. In a small mixing bowl, combine the 1 tablespoon sugar and cinnamon. Sprinkle over the warm crepes. Serve immediately. Makes 24 roll-ups (8 to 12 servings).
Chunky Applesauce: Peel, core, and cut into wedges 2 or 3 Golden Delicious, Northern Spy, or Mutsu *apples* (about 1 pound). In a small saucepan, combine apples and 2 tablespoons *water.* Bring to boiling; reduce heat. Cover tightly and simmer for 8 to 10 minutes or till tender. Slightly mash apple. Use immediately for roll-ups. Makes 1¼ cups.

Grandma Teichman's Apple Dressing

Herb Teichman recalls the aroma of this dressing from his grandmother's kitchen. The side dish (not a stuffing) is more apple than bread. It's especially good with pork or duck.

- 2 cups soft bread crumbs
- 4 cups chopped, unpeeled apple
  (4 medium apples)
- 3 stalks celery, finely chopped
- 1 small onion, finely chopped
- ¼ cup raisins
- ¼ cup packed brown sugar
- 1 teaspoon ground cinnamon
- ½ teaspoon salt
- ¼ cup butter or *margarine, melted*

1. In a shallow baking pan, toast bread crumbs in a 350° oven for 8 to 10 minutes or till lightly browned.
2. In a large bowl, combine apple, celery, onion, raisins, brown sugar, cinnamon, and salt. Drizzle butter or margarine over all; toss till well mixed. Add bread crumbs; toss till combined.
3. Spoon into a lightly greased 2-quart casserole. Bake, covered, in a 350° oven for 40 to 45 minutes or till apples are tender. Uncover and bake about 5 minutes to brown top. Makes 8 to 10 servings.

Glazed Fresh Apple Cookies

Each fall the Teichmans look forward to these big, spicy treats that are loaded with delicious fruit and nuts.

1⅓ cups packed brown sugar
½ cup shortening
1 egg
2 cups all-purpose flour
1 teaspoon baking soda
1 teaspoon ground cinnamon
¼ teaspoon salt
¼ teaspoon ground cloves
¼ cup apple juice *or* apple cider
1½ cups chopped, unpeeled apple
  (1 large apple)
1 cup chopped nuts
1 cup raisins
1½ cups sifted powdered sugar
2 tablespoons milk
1 tablespoon butter *or* margarine,
  softened
¼ teaspoon vanilla
  Dash salt

1. In a mixing bowl, beat brown sugar and shortening with an electric mixer on medium speed till well combined. Beat in egg till fluffy. In a bowl, combine flour, baking soda, cinnamon, the ¼ teaspoon salt, and cloves. Beat into creamed mixture on low speed. Beat in apple juice or cider. By hand, stir in apple, nuts, and raisins.
2. Drop dough by slightly rounded tablespoons onto a greased cookie sheet. Bake in a 400° oven for 7 to 8 minutes or till edges are golden.
3. Meanwhile, in a small bowl, combine the powdered sugar, milk, butter or margarine, vanilla, and the dash salt. Stir the mixture till smooth. Spread on warm cookies. Makes 36.

Liz Teichman's Glazed Fresh Apple Cookies and Brandied Apple Roll-Ups, and Grandma's Apple Dressing.

Mini Crepes

Fill these light and tender crepes with an apple mixture for Brandied Apple Roll-Ups (see recipe, page 46) or wrap them around other fruit fillings.

½ cup milk
½ cup all-purpose flour
¼ cup sugar
3 egg yolks
3 tablespoons butter or *margarine,*
   melted
¼ teaspoon vanilla
3 egg whites

1. In a medium bowl, beat together milk, flour, sugar, egg yolks, butter or margarine, and vanilla.
2. In a large mixing bowl, beat egg whites with an electric mixer on high speed till stiff peaks form (tips stand straight). Gently fold yolk mixture into the beaten egg whites.
3. Heat a lightly greased 6-inch skillet. Remove from heat. Spoon in *1 slightly rounded tablespoon* of batter; spread batter with back of spoon or lift and tilt skillet to spread batter to a 4-inch circle. Cook over medium heat for 30 to 60 seconds or till underside is browned and surface is almost dry. Loosen with a metal spatula and invert onto paper towels. Repeat with remaining batter. (Stir batter gently as necessary.) Use crepes immediately or freeze. Makes 24 crepes.
To Freeze Crepes: Make a stack, alternating each layer with 2 layers of waxed paper. Place the stack in a moisture- and vapor-proof plastic bag. Seal, label, and freeze the crepes for up to 4 months. Let the crepes thaw at room temperature for 1 hour before using.

Dianne Rentschler and Susan Rentschler Wright bake Apple Pastry Squares and Apple Pudding with Rummy Sauce.

Apple Pastry Squares

1½ cups sugar
1 teaspoon ground cinnamon
½ teaspoon ground nutmeg
8 cups sliced, peeled cooking apples
    (7 large apples)
4 cups all-purpose flour
1½ cups shortening
2 beaten eggs
6 tablespoons water
¼ cup lemon juice
2 tablespoons butter or margarine
    Powdered Sugar Icing

1. In an extra large bowl, combine sugar, cinnamon, and nutmeg. Add apple slices; toss to coat.
2. In another extra large bowl, mix the flour and 1½ teaspoons *salt*. With a pastry blender, cut in the shortening till pieces are the size of small peas. In a small bowl, combine eggs, water, and lemon juice. Add to flour mixture; mix till moistened. Divide in half.
3. On a lightly floured surface, roll *half* of the dough into a 16x11-inch rectangle. Ease pastry into a 15x10x1-inch baking pan (should be a ½-inch pastry border around pan).
4. Drain apple mixture, if necessary. Arrange apple mixture evenly over the pastry in the pan. Dot with butter or margarine. Roll out remaining dough to a 15½x10½-inch rectangle. Fit pastry over apple mixture. Seal and crimp pastry edges together. Cut several slits in top pastry.
5. To prevent overbrowning, cover edge of pastry with foil. Bake in a 375° oven for 25 minutes. Remove foil. Bake for 15 to 20 minutes more or till golden. Drizzle icing over hot pastry. To serve, cut pastry into squares. Makes 12 to 16 servings.
Powdered Sugar Icing: In a bowl, combine 1 cup sifted *powdered sugar* and 2 tablespoons *milk*.

Apple Pudding with Rummy Sauce

Creamy rum sauce tops this warm, homey pudding, but generous scoops of ice cream are compatible, too.

¼ cup butter or margarine
1 cup sugar
1 egg
1 cup all-purpose flour
1 teaspoon baking soda
¾ teaspoon ground nutmeg
¼ teaspoon salt
4 cups chopped, unpeeled apple
    (4 medium apples)
¼ cup chopped pecans
    Rummy Sauce

1. In a large mixing bowl, beat butter or margarine with an electric mixer on medium speed for 30 seconds. Add sugar; beat till well combined. Add egg; beat well. In a small bowl, combine flour, baking soda, nutmeg, and salt. Add to creamed mixture. Beat on low speed till combined.
2. By hand, fold apple and pecans into batter. Spread in a greased 8x8x2-inch baking pan.
3. Bake in a 350° oven about 55 minutes or till golden brown. Cut into 9 squares. Serve warm with Rummy Sauce. Makes 9 servings.
Rummy Sauce: In a small saucepan, melt ½ cup *butter or margarine*. Stir in 1 cup *sugar* and ½ cup light *cream*. Bring just to boiling over medium heat. Reduce heat and cook for 3 minutes, stirring occasionally. Remove from heat. Stir in 2 tablespoons *rum*, 1 teaspoon ground *nutmeg*, and 1 teaspoon *vanilla*. Spoon over warm pudding. Makes about 1½ cups sauce.

Hop on! Half the fun of apple picking for regulars or first-timers is getting to the orchard.

49

Apple Pie à la Mode

Apple Pie à la Mode

This all-American favorite dessert is pictured on the cover.

1 cup sugar
3 tablespoons all-purpose flour
1 teaspoon ground cinnamon
6 cups thinly sliced, peeled, cooking
   apples (about 2 pounds)
1 tablespoon lemon juice
   Pastry
2 tablespoons butter or margarine
1 egg yolk
2 tablespoons milk
1 tablespoon sugar
   Vanilla ice cream

1. In a bowl, combine the 1 cup sugar, flour, and cinnamon. Add apples and lemon juice; toss to coat apples.
2. On a lightly floured surface, roll out 1 ball of Pastry to fit a 9-inch pie plate. Trim pastry ½ inch beyond edge of pie plate. Roll out remaining Pastry. Cut into ½-inch-wide strips.
3. Spoon the apple mixture into the pastry-lined pie plate. Dot with butter or margarine.
4. Weave pastry strips over apple filling to make a lattice crust. Press ends of strips into rim of bottom crust. Fold bottom pastry over strips. Seal and crimp edge.
5. Beat together the egg yolk and milk. Brush over pastry. Sprinkle with the 1 tablespoon sugar.
6. Cover pie loosely with foil. Bake in a 375° oven for 35 minutes. Remove foil and bake for 30 to 35 minutes more or till the top is golden and apples are tender. Cool slightly on a wire rack. Serve slices of pie warm with ice cream. Makes 8 servings.
Pastry: In a bowl, combine 2 cups *all-purpose flour* and ½ teaspoon *salt*. Cut in ⅔ cup *shortening* till pieces are the size of small peas. Add ⅓ cup *cold water*, about 1 tablespoon at a time, tossing with a fork till all is moistened. Form dough into 2 balls.

Nuts to You From Iowa

Indian summer sends Heartlanders on nutting safaris. Learn the secrets from a wily Iowa nutter.

On most sunny autumn afternoons, you'll find Jack Hawn at his favorite nutting grounds, a farm in a scenic setting along Iowa's Racoon River. He'll be gathering black walnuts in 5-gallon buckets and hefting them into the back of his pickup. "I collect nuts for an hour or so," Jack explains with a smile. "Then, I sit on the tailgate and enjoy the sun. If I had to hurry, I'd quit."

Since his grandkids gave him a bushel of black walnuts a few years ago, Jack has been hooked. He cracked those nuts and wound up with 4 quarts of nutmeats and a hobby he really loves.

Jack took up nutting in earnest after retiring from his own service station in his hometown of Perry, Iowa (40 miles northwest of Des Moines). Now, at 73, he gathers walnuts in the fall and cranks his one-of-a-kind cracker all winter.

WALNUT PARTICULARS

Knowing where to find the most prolific trees that bear the best-tasting nuts is the key to nutting success, and that's a cinch for Jack. He and his wife, Marville, grew up here. They know where the best trees are and who owns them.

But Jack still does on-the-spot taste testing. He carries a hammer and, before wasting time gathering, taps a nut open and takes a bite. The thinner the shell, he explains, the more nutmeat.

Jack also looks for black walnuts that have soft hulls. "Give 'em a little squeeze, and you usually can tell if there's a good walnut inside," he claims. (Hard hulls can mean no nutmeats.)

After he finishes gathering, Jack hauls his buckets of black walnuts to nearby Beaver, Iowa, where they're mechanically husked.

Jack washes the nuts in (are you ready for this?) an old electric Maytag washer that he and a neighbor rigged up in his backyard. His formula: 5 gallons of nuts and 5 gallons of water for an 8- to 10-minute cycle. "The less water, the cleaner they get," says Jack, explaining how friction helps clean the nuts.

Then, Jack dries the nuts in a 10-inch-deep, squirrel-proof screened box he built from an old door screen. He puts the box in the shade, so the nuts don't dry too fast and shrink the meats. "You can tell when they're dry enough," claims Jack. "The nuts kind of rattle."

Jack hangs up the dried black walnuts in mesh bags in his basement—the hub of his

For nutter Jack Hawn, experience and a home in walnut country spell success.

nutcracking operation. With a surgeon's skill, he opens the shells one by one, using the trusted nutcracker that he bought and adapted (it's a gear-driven giz-whiz Jack cranks by hand).

Along with his other nutting inventions, Jack created a chicken-wire soaker that looks like a giant french-fry basket that fits inside a bucket. (Black walnuts crack better after soaking.)

THE NUTTER'S CREDO

Jack's formula for keeping other nutters away from the trees he likes seems to work. "The best way to guard a good tree," says Jack, "Is to give the person who owns it a couple of sacks of nuts right before Christmas."

Patting his Santa Claus waistline, this seasoned nutter admits he nibbles as he cracks the black walnuts. That's the best part of nutting—eating the harvest. Jack's refrigerator bulges with bags of golden nutmeats, and his freezer stores a surplus—just in case there's a bad year.

Jack's favorite delicacy? Marville's Marvelous Maple-Nut Ice Cream, which Marville says tastes best served with her Chocolate-on-Chocolate Walnut Cookies (see recipes, opposite).

Nut-Hunting Know-How

In the Midwest, nutting season usually runs from mid-September through late October. Plan to get an early start, lest the squirrels—and various two-legged nutters—beat you to the bounty. Besides black walnuts like the ones Jack Hawn gathers, hickory nuts, butternuts, chestnuts, and pecans grow in our region. In colder northern Midwest states, walnuts and hazelnuts (also called filberts) do best, while pecans and hicans (a cross between a hickory nut and a pecan) thrive in the Midwest's southern reaches. Jack offers novice hunters this advice:

❖ Ask permission from property owners before you start gathering.
❖ Gather nuts off the ground; never pick them from trees. When nuts are ripe, they drop.
❖ Choose the medium-size black walnuts you find. Small nuts make cracking a chore, and large nuts are more likely to have thick shells and little nutmeat.
❖ Husk the black walnuts right away to reduce staining of the nutmeats and to prevent a bitter taste.

Wear gloves when you work with black walnuts to keep the stain from the shells off your hands.
❖ If you don't have an old Maytag around like Jack does, you can wash nuts in a bucket of water. Use a stick to stir the nuts and agitate the water.
❖ Discard nuts that float to the surface during washing—they're probably empty. (This test works when nuts are husked and washed right after collecting.)

❖ An old window screen or door screen makes a good drying box. Spread the nuts on it in a well-ventilated spot out of reach of neighborhood squirrels.
❖ Old mesh onion bags or potato sacks make good storage containers for air-dried black walnuts.
❖ Before cracking, soak nuts in water for 48 to 56 hours. Then, let the uncracked nuts dry for about 10 hours. The nutmeats will crack out in bigger pieces.
❖ When cracking nuts with a hammer, tap each nut on its head (right where all the sides meet) to lay the nut open in two pieces.
❖ The nutmeat's skin color is a clue to storage expectancy. Dark-skinned nutmeats often shrivel quickly; light-skinned nutmeats keep longer.
❖ Refrigerate your nutmeats in plastic bags or airtight containers for several weeks. Or, freeze nutmeats in freezer containers for up to a year.

Chocolate-on-Chocolate Walnut Cookies

Celebrate fall with these moist, nut-crunchy cookies crowned with swirls of creamy chocolate frosting.

2¾ cups all-purpose flour
½ teaspoon baking soda
½ teaspoon baking powder
¼ teaspoon salt
1½ cups sugar
½ cup butter or margarine
2 eggs
1 teaspoon vanilla
2 squares (2 ounces) unsweetened chocolate, melted and cooled
1 cup dairy sour cream
1 cup coarsely chopped black walnuts
Chocolate-Cream Cheese Frosting (optional)

1. In a bowl, combine flour, baking soda, baking powder, and salt.
2. In a large mixer bowl, cream sugar and butter or margarine on low speed of electric mixer. Add eggs and vanilla; beat on medium speed till fluffy.
3. Beat in cooled, melted chocolate and sour cream. Add flour mixture; beat on low speed till well-mixed.
4. With a spoon, stir in black walnuts. Cover; chill for 1 hour.
5. From a teaspoon, drop dough 2 inches apart onto a greased cookie sheet. Bake in a 375° oven for 8 to 10 minutes. Transfer cookies to a wire rack; cool. Frost with Chocolate-Cream Cheese Frosting, if desired. Store frosted cookies in the refrigerator. Makes about 60.

Chocolate-Cream Cheese Frosting: In a mixer bowl, beat together till light and fluffy one 3-ounce package *cream cheese*, softened; 2 tablespoons *butter or margarine*, softened; 1½ squares (1½ ounces) *unsweetened chocolate*, melted and cooled; 2 tablespoons *milk or light cream*; and ½ teaspoon *vanilla*. Gradually add 2 cups sifted *powdered sugar*, beating till smooth. Add a little more milk or powdered sugar, if necessary to make mixture a spreading consistency.

Marville's Marvelous Maple-Nut Ice Cream

Make a freezer of Marville Hawn's homemade maple-nut ice cream and you'll be licking the dasher, just as her husband, Jack, does.

3 cups light cream
1½ cups sugar
2 tablespoons maple flavoring
1 tablespoon vanilla
3 cups whipping cream
¾ cup chopped black walnuts

1. In the freezer can of a 4- to 5-quart ice cream freezer, combine light cream, sugar, maple flavoring, and vanilla. Stir the mixture till the sugar is dissolved.
2. Stir in whipping cream and black walnuts. Freeze mixture according to manufacturer's directions. Makes 2 quarts.
Note: For a 2-quart ice cream freezer, use ⅔ of the recipe above and freeze according to manufacturer's directions.

Serve Marville's Marvelous Maple-Nut Ice Cream with Chocolate-on-Chocolate Walnut Cookies.

"The best way to guard a good tree," says Jack, "is to give the person who owns it a couple of sacks of nuts right before Christmas."

BRING ON THE BERRIES
Sweet Pickin's

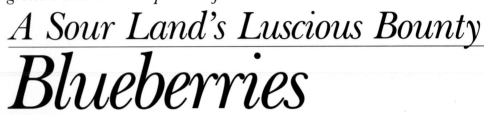

You pick 'em, you eat 'em! That sounds like a deliciously fair proposition—and fun, especially when you visit the Midwest's outstanding you-pick berry farms. Besides bringing home the berries, you'll meet some of the region's expert growers and even sample their families' favorite berry recipes.

A Sour Land's Luscious Bounty
Blueberries

As he strolls the fragrant ranks of chest-high bushes at DeGrandchamp Blueberry Farm, Vince DeGrandchamp's weathered hand delicately plucks a couple of frosty-blue berries and pops them into his mouth. "This is about the only time I eat 'em," he grins.

Of course, the patriarch of the DeGrandchamp clan spends much of each summer day amid the 100 acres of bushes on his family farm southeast of South Haven, Michigan. And that translates into a lot of blueberry munching.

When the you-pick-'em sign goes up in early July, Vince has plenty of company. Folks with visions of blueberry flapjacks and ice cream stream in from as far south as Chicago, a 2½-hour drive, and from as far east as Grand Rapids, an hour's drive.

Even a novice needs only a few minutes to fill one of the blue, gallon-size harvest buckets. "They're easy picking, really," promises Vince's son Joe.

Both Joe, and brother Mike, are Vince's partners. And all their families help out. The you-pick-'em operation is a pleasant sideline to a sophisticated business that, through the Michigan Blueberry Growers Association, sells thousands of pounds of berries, both fresh and processed as jams, syrups, and other products.

Vince's pride and joy are the farm's mechanical pickers, huge Rube Goldberg-ish machines that straddle a row and gently jiggle the delicate berries from the bushes. Berries that must arrive on the

(From left) Vince and Bea; Martha, holding Nicholas, and Mike; Judy DeGrand-champ Johnson with Sarah and Carmen; Bob, Kate, and Joe.

grocer's shelf in perfect condition still are picked by hand.

The spread included only about a dozen acres of blueberries when Vince, a farm kid turned electrician, bought it three decades ago, moving his family from Detroit. Back then, many people still picked wild berries that grew in the sour soil of Great Lakes-region bogs and swamps.

The DeGrandchamp farm soil is perfect for blueberries—sandy and acidic. "It's useless soil," says Joe. "But blueberries love it."

If you want to try raising blueberries, Joe recommends souring the soil (add sulfur). Or, grow the bushes in Canadian peat moss in raised beds or containers. Moist, well-drained soil is best. The Bluecrop variety is Joe's mainstay, but he also favors compact, heavy-bearing Blueray bushes.

Blueberry-picking season extends from early July into mid-August. For more information, contact *DeGrandchamp's Blueberry Farm, 15575 77th St., South Haven, MI 49090 (616/637-3915).*

Milk Chocolate Blueberry Clusters

Bea DeGrandchamp says these confections are just one of many imaginative ways to eat blueberries.

1 11½-ounce package milk chocolate pieces
¼ cup shortening
2 cups fresh blueberries, rinsed and drained well

1. In a heavy saucepan over low heat or in the top of a double boiler set over hot water, melt milk chocolate pieces and shortening. Stir till smooth. Remove from heat.
2. Gently fold in blueberries till well coated. Drop by teaspoon into 1¼- to 1½-inch paper candy cups or onto a baking sheet lined with waxed paper.
3. Chill in refrigerator for 20 to 30 minutes or till chocolate is set. Candies can be kept at room temperature for about 1 hour. If chocolate becomes soft and sticky, return to refrigerator. Store in refrigerator for up to 24 hours. Makes about 36 candies.
White Blueberry Clusters: Follow directions for Milk Chocolate Blueberry Clusters, *except* substitute 12 ounces *white baking bars with cocoa butter,* cut up, for milk chocolate.
To use your microwave oven: Place the milk chocolate pieces or the cut-up white baking bars and shortening into a 1½-quart microwave-safe bowl. Micro-cook, uncovered, on 100% power (high) for 1½ to 2½ minutes or just till the mixture becomes smooth when stirred. Complete the candy as above.

Milk Chocolate and White Blueberry Clusters

Blueberry-Sour Cream Cake

Served warm from the oven, this cinnamony, blueberry-blessed cake is a DeGrandchamp family favorite.

2 cups all-purpose flour
1 teaspoon baking soda
1 teaspoon salt
1 cup packed brown sugar
1 cup chopped nuts
1 teaspoon ground cinnamon
½ cup butter or *margarine*
1 cup sugar
1 teaspoon vanilla
3 eggs
1 8-ounce carton dairy sour cream
2 cups fresh blueberries or *frozen, unsweetened blueberries, partially thawed*

1. In a medium bowl, stir together flour, baking soda, and salt; set aside. In a second bowl, combine brown sugar, nuts, and cinnamon; set aside.
2. In a large mixer bowl, beat butter or margarine with an electric mixer on medium speed for 30 seconds. Add sugar and vanilla; beat till fluffy. Add eggs, one at a time, beating well after each addition. Beat in sour cream. Add flour mixture; beat till smooth. By hand, fold in blueberries.
3. Spread *half* of the batter in a greased 13x9x2-inch baking pan. Sprinkle *half* of the brown sugar mixture evenly over batter. Dollop remaining batter on top; spread slightly. Sprinkle remaining brown sugar mixture over surface of batter.
4. Bake in a 350° oven for 45 to 50 minutes or till done. Serve warm or cooled. Makes 12 to 16 servings.

Blueberry-Cream Cheese Fingers

Bea DeGrandchamp shared the secret of these pastries. Inside each is a lineup of blueberries.

1 cup butter, softened
1 8-ounce package cream cheese, softened
2 cups all-purpose flour
2 tablespoons sugar
1 tablespoon all-purpose flour
1 tablespoon sugar
1 cup fresh blueberries or *frozen, unsweetened blueberries, thawed*
1 beaten egg yolk
1 tablespoon water

1. In a mixer bowl, cream butter and cream cheese with an electric mixer till well blended. In a small bowl, combine the 2 cups flour and 2 tablespoons sugar; beat into butter mixture. Divide pastry in half and shape into 2 balls. Wrap each ball in waxed paper or clear plastic wrap. Chill for 1 to 2 hours or till easy to handle.
2. Meanwhile, in a shallow plate, combine the 1 tablespoon flour and 1 tablespoon sugar. Roll blueberries in mixture.
3. On a lightly floured surface, roll *one* ball of the pastry into a 25x10-inch rectangle. Cut into ten 5-inch squares. On each square near an edge, arrange 8 to 10 coated blueberries in a row. Roll up pastry, jelly-roll style; pinch ends together. Place on an ungreased cookie sheet, seam side down. Repeat with the remaining dough and blueberries.
4. In a small bowl, combine egg yolk and water; brush onto the tops of pastries. Bake the pastries in a 350° oven for about 20 minutes. Makes 20 pastries.

Blueberry-Cream Cheese Fingers

A Feast for Creatures Great and Small
Strawberries

Tom Miller has been eating, learning about, and growing strawberries ever since he was a child tending his parents' berry patch.

Some of the most skilled you-pick-'em devotees that flock to Miller Strawberry Acres each June are the deer and songbirds that live nearby in Wisconsin's wooded Rib River bottomland.

Who can blame them? Tom Miller's farm west of Wausau is a strawberry lover's dream: acre upon acre of plump berries basking in the sun. "We've used noisemakers and all sorts of stuff," Tom says in his quiet, country-boy way of attempts to shoo off the berry snatchers. "I guess we just have to put up with them."

But don't worry. Between Strawberry Acres and M & M Berries, a second farm 20 miles north, about 30 acres ripen each spring. During the season's week-long peak in mid to late June, up to 2,000 pickers hunker over the rows by noon each day. Tom hires a pair of parking attendants just to control the traffic.

Since childhood, Tom has been learning the secrets of strawberry growing. He helped tend the sizable patch on his parents' dairy farm. When his father suffered a heart attack, Tom took over the farm instead of heading for college and a career in meteorology. He began to edge out of the dairy business and into strawberries full time. Now, Tom operates the two farms with partner Joan Burk-Miller.

"Things have a way of working out," says Tom. He and his wife Barbara live in a home Tom designed and built of red-pine logs from Michigan's Upper Peninsula. The house overlooks a 26-acre lake stocked with trout. But, despite the idyllic setting, Tom manages to keep busy.

Since strawberry plants set few berries their first year and stop producing heavily after the fourth year, Tom replants part of his crop each spring to ensure good picking. The toughest chore, often tackled by local high-school kids, is handpicking blossoms off young plants, forcing the plants to develop good roots. Usually, that job must be done twice during each plant's first season.

Tom sticks with June-bearing strawberries. He recommends Honeoye, an early variety ("A very, very good-quality berry," Tom promises) and Blomidon, a large, tasty Canadian berry that winters well. A thick mulch of marsh hay helps Tom's plants weather Wisconsin winters.

Tom's berries usually begin to ripen about June 15; picking lasts three to four weeks. For more information, call the seasonal Strawberry Hot Line *(715/842-4000)* at *Miller Strawberry Acres, 908 S. 48th Ave., Wausau, WI 54401.* M & M Berries is 5 miles north of Merrill on State-107 N (call 715/536-4027).

Tom Miller and Joan Burk-Miller tempt pickers with about 30 acres of June berries.

Strawberry-Wine Slush

This pretty refresher, which you can mix up in a jiffy, is a favorite of Joan Burk-Miller. Each year, Joan treats customers to a brochure loaded with such strawberry recipes and information—printed on pink paper, of course.

½ pint fresh strawberries
⅔ cup sauterne
½ of a 6-ounce can frozen limeade
    concentrate
8 large ice cubes
   Sugar (optional)

1. In a blender container, combine the fresh strawberries, sauterne, frozen limeade concentrate, and ice cubes. Blend till the mixture is smooth. Add sugar, if a sweeter flavor is desired.
2. Serve immediately in stemmed glasses. Makes about 2½ cups of slush (five 4-ounce servings).
Note: Slush may be transferred to a plastic container, covered, and frozen. Store in the freezer for up to 4 weeks.

Strawberry-Spinach Salad

When Joan Burk-Miller hosted a luncheon for Alice in Dairyland contenders at Miller Strawberry Acres, she devised a menu of mostly nonfattening foods. Her salad is elegant enough for any royalty.

6 cups torn fresh spinach (8 ounces)
½ teaspoon toasted sesame seed
2 cups fresh strawberries
¼ cup salad oil (not olive oil)
2 tablespoons red wine vinegar
1½ tablespoons sugar
1½ teaspoons snipped fresh dillweed or
    ½ teaspoon dried dillweed
⅛ teaspoon salt
⅛ teaspoon onion powder
⅛ teaspoon garlic powder
⅛ teaspoon dry mustard
⅛ teaspoon pepper

1. Place spinach in a large bowl. Sprinkle with toasted sesame seed. Cut large strawberries in half; add berries to salad.
2. In a screw-top jar, combine salad oil, red wine vinegar, sugar, dillweed, salt, onion powder, garlic powder, dry mustard, and pepper. Cover; shake. (Dressing may be prepared several hours before serving; chill. Shake well before using.)
3. Pour dressing over mixture in bowl; toss gently. Makes 6 servings.

(Top) Strawberry-Wine Slush. (Right) Strawberry-Spinach Salad.

Strawberries
In Petal Cups

Strawberry grower Joan Burk-Miller likes to present strawberries in different ways. So, sometimes she serves the unexpected, such as this dessert with its savory and sweet flavors.

1 cup shredded process Swiss cheese
   (4 ounces), at room temperature
¼ cup butter, softened
½ cup all-purpose flour
2 cups sliced fresh strawberries
3 tablespoons strawberry liqueur or
   sugar
½ cup whipping cream, whipped
   (optional)

1. In a mixer bowl, beat the shredded process Swiss cheese and the butter on medium speed of an electric mixer till smooth. Stir in the flour till all is incorporated. Shape into an 8-inch-long roll. Wrap in waxed paper or clear plastic wrap; chill pastry for about 2 hours or till it's firm enough to slice.
2. Line 8 muffin cups with foil. Grease the foil and top of the pan well. Cut the chilled pastry roll into 48 slices, about ⅛ inch thick (6 slices per inch). For each pastry cup, place 1 pastry slice in the bottom of the muffin cup. Arrange 5 slices around the side of the cup, overlapping slightly.
3. Bake the pastry cups in a 375° oven for 12 to 14 minutes or till they're lightly browned. Cool the pastries in the muffin cups on wire racks for 5 minutes; carefully remove the pastry cups from the muffin cups by lifting the foil edges. Cool the pastries completely. Gently peel the foil off pastry cups.
4. For the filling, about 30 minutes before serving, combine the

Strawberries in Petal Cups

strawberries and strawberry liqueur or sugar. Cover and chill the mixture.
5. To serve, divide the strawberries and the strawberry liquid among the pastry cups, using about ¼ cup berries for each cup. Top with whipped cream, if desired. Makes 8 servings.

Choosing Berries

Ten of the most popular varieties of berries are listed in the chart below. You'll find a few of the berries, such as strawberries and blueberries, sold in supermarkets. Check roadside stands and farmer's markets for the other berries, which usually are locally grown.

SELECTING
Choose berries with good color for the variety. If picking your own, select berries that separate easily from their stems. Avoid bruised or moldy fruit.

STORING
Refrigerate berries in a single layer, loosely covered. Avoid heaping them in a bowl or container because this will crush the delicate fruit. Use most berries within a day or two.

To freeze the fruit, arrange washed berries, with stems removed, on a baking sheet. Place in the freezer until solid; transfer the frozen berries to plastic freezer containers or bags, leaving ½-inch headspace. Return to the freezer.

Berry varieties differ in texture, skin color, and sweetness. How berries are used depends on their sweetness. Naturally sweet berries, such as strawberries, can be eaten raw, often without sweetening. Tart and sour berries, such as cranberries and gooseberries, usually are served sweetened with sugar and cooked.

Type	Color	Qualities	Flavor
BLACKBERRY	*Purplish black to black*	Soft, juicy	*Sweet, tangy*
BLUEBERRY	*Purplish blue*	Plump, firm	*Mildly sweet*
CRANBERRY	*Glossy red*	Plump, firm	*Tart*
CURRANT	*Red, white, or black*	Firm	*Tart, tangy*
ELDERBERRY	*Deep purple to black*	Soft, juicy	*Sweet*
GOOSEBERRY	*Pale green*	Crisp	*Tart*
LINGONBERRY	*Dark red*	Firm	*Very tart*
MULBERRY	*Bluish purple, red, reddish black, or nearly white*	Soft	*Mildly sweet to slightly sour*
RASPBERRY	*Red, golden, or black*	Soft	*Mildly sweet*
STRAWBERRY	*Bright red*	Soft	*Mildly sweet*

Harvesting a North Woods Delicacy

A late summer breeze shoos the mosquitoes away. Hats and bandanas bob in the early sun. Only hungry mallards, dipping down for breakfast in the watery rice beds, break the silence of the aspen backwoods.

Crouched in the hull of her canoe, veteran ricer Wanda Patzoldt scouts the horizon for ripe rice. Her husband Arnold poles their craft north across Minnesota's Bass Lake, gliding toward the green-gold stalks that Wanda bends with her wooden flails. Then she beats the ripe, grainlike seeds into the canoe.

The Grand Rapids, Minnesota, couple are old hands at this ritual they've practiced for more than 29 years. Arnold and Wanda take a break from their bakery and wild-rice/maple-syrup mail-order business. Together, they spend part of every late summer afloat.

"Ricing is like panning for gold," Wanda explains. "Once it gets in your blood, you can't quit."

TALES OF INDIAN RICE WARS

Mert Lego and his Chippewa friends at nearby Leech Lake Indian Reservation couldn't agree more. "The Chippewa have thrived on wild rice for generations. They've feuded over it, too," Mert says, recalling tales of the 1700s, when his people and the Sioux battled over Minnesota's rice-rich waters.

As summer wanes in Minnesota's lake country, dedicated ricers gather their precious harvest by hand. Meet some experts and try these tantalizing wild rice recipes.

Arnold Patzoldt skillfully guides his canoe through a wild-rice bed, as his wife Wanda eyes green-gold stalks of ripe wild rice ready to harvest.

Today, the much-anticipated ricing season arrives peacefully at Leech Lake, but the nearly 5,000 Chippewa who live at the reservation still take their wild rice seriously. After bringing in canoes laden with wild rice, the Chippewa stow away plenty for their winter larders and sell the rest off the reservation.

"We never get tired of eating rice," assures Mert. "Most of us just boil it with bacon or salt pork."

WORLD-CLASS RICERS

Minnesota and California rank as the nation's largest producers of wild rice. On a much smaller scale, northern Wisconsin also draws ricers (in the Webster, Hayward, and Manitowish Waters areas).

While the Chippewa and some wild-rice purists like the Patzoldts still flail away from canoes in shallow lake beds and marshy bogs, most of Minnesota's rice grows in man-made paddies. Giant harvesting machines— contraptions that resemble hybrids of combines and Caterpillar tractors— gobble up the crop on land unsuited to other farming.

But the Patzoldts aren't about to abandon their old-fashioned ways. "We prefer harvesting the rice ourselves," Wanda says. "It's just like the difference between picking wild blueberries and going to the store and buying them."

To order Wanda's wild rice, write: *Lost Frontier, 3001 Horseshoe Lake Rd., Grand Rapids, MN 55744.*

Celebration Casserole

Prepare this easy-does-it creation from the north woods for company or memorable family feasts.

1 cup sliced fresh mushrooms
¼ cup chopped onion
¼ cup chopped celery
¼ cup chopped green pepper
1 clove garlic, minced
¼ cup margarine or butter, melted
3 cups Cooked Wild Rice (see recipe, right)
½ cup slivered almonds, toasted
½ cup shredded cheddar cheese (2 ounces)
Dash pepper

1. In a medium saucepan, cook the mushrooms, onion, celery, green pepper, and garlic in margarine or butter till vegetables are tender.
2. In a 2-quart casserole combine the cooked wild rice, vegetable mixture, almonds, cheddar cheese, and pepper.
3. Cover and bake in a 325° oven for 40 to 45 minutes or till casserole is heated through. Makes 8 servings.

Celebration Casserole (opposite, left)
Chippewa Muffins (opposite, right)

Cooked Wild Rice

Serve wild rice as a side dish with meat, fish, and poultry, or use it as an ingredient in other recipes.

1 cup wild rice
2½ cups beef broth, chicken broth, or water
¼ teaspoon salt

1. Run cold water over the rice in a strainer for about 1 minute, lifting the rice to rinse it thoroughly.
2. In a saucepan, stir together the rice, broth or water, and salt. Bring mixture to boiling. Reduce heat. Cover and simmer for 40 to 45 minutes or till done and most of the liquid is absorbed from the rice. Drain off any excess liquid.
3. Fluff the cooked wild rice with a fork. Serve hot or store the rice, covered, in the refrigerator for up to 5 days. You also can pack the rice in a freezer container, seal, label, and freeze. Makes about 3 cups of wild rice (6 servings).

Chippewa Muffins

Wild rice transforms these otherwise ordinary muffins into a distinctive and delicious bread.

1¾ cups all-purpose flour
¼ cup sugar
2 teaspoons baking powder
½ teaspoon salt
1 beaten egg
1 cup Cooked Wild Rice, cooled (see recipe, left)
¾ cup milk
⅓ cup cooking oil

1. In a large mixing bowl, stir together flour, sugar, baking powder, and salt. Make a well in the center.
2. In another mixing bowl, combine the egg, Cooked Wild Rice, milk, and cooking oil. Add all at once to the flour mixture. Stir just till moistened. The batter should be lumpy.
3. Grease muffin cups or line with paper bake cups; fill each cup ⅔ full. Bake in a 400° oven for 20 to 25 minutes or till muffins are golden. Makes 10 to 12 muffins.

Wild Rice Facts

Long ago dubbed "rice" because it grows in water, wild rice is not a rice at all. Rather, it is the seed of an annual marsh grass and is the only cereal grain native to North America.

Uncooked wild rice keeps indefinitely stored in a cool, dry place or in the refrigerator. If it is cooked with no added ingredients, wild rice keeps, tightly covered, in the refrigerator for several days or in the freezer for several months.

Nutty-flavored wild rice is delicious on its own or combined with white or brown rice to make a flavorful pilaf.

North Dakota Sunflower Sensations

Swaying fields of platter-size flowers dot the Plains States—from the Dakotas to Kansas. Try these surprising North Dakota sunflower specialties.

Anyone who pulls up a chair at the Sunflower Cafe in Grace City, North Dakota, probably won't get out the door without hearing about sunflowers. Why all the sunflower commotion? The local elevator does a bang-up business in the flowers and their kernels each year, and the farmers and folks who work there are regulars at the cafe. Because their livelihood depends at least in part on sunflowers, cafe patrons are quite often chitchatting about the flowers.

The cafe menu once touted a long list of sunflower dishes, including cookies, pies, and malts. Today, sunflower offerings aren't as popular as they once were. But every once in a while, the cafe serves its thick sunflower malts and famous North Dakota Sunflower Pie (see recipe, right). Created by retired cafe manager Alice Scranson, this pie has a pecan-pie-like flavor and texture. It's described by sunflower aficionados as "so-o-o rich."

SPREADING THE SUNFLOWER GOSPEL

While the cafe serves thick malts and slices of sinful pie, sunflower boosters all over North and South Dakota promote new ways for cooks to use sunflower products.

For instance, you'll find Ardith Zimbleman handing out sunflower recipes almost anywhere folks get together, including the state fair. She and her husband cultivate about 800 acres of sunflowers every year on their farm near Fullerton, North Dakota.

"I substitute sunflower kernels for nuts in almost any recipe," Ardith says. "You can make almost anything with them." Ardith passed along her recipe for Sun Crunchies (see recipe, opposite), from the National Sunflower Association.

North Dakota Sunflower Pie

    3 beaten eggs
    ½ cup packed brown sugar
    ½ cup light corn syrup
    ½ cup dark corn syrup
    ¼ cup sugar
    3 tablespoons sunflower margarine,
         melted
    1 teaspoon vanilla
    ¼ teaspoon salt
    1 cup roasted, salted sunflower kernels
    1 unbaked 9-inch pie shell

1. In a large bowl, beat together eggs, brown sugar, corn syrups, sugar, margarine, vanilla, and salt.
2. Spread sunflower kernels evenly in the bottom of the unbaked pie shell. Pour in the sugar mixture.
3. Bake in a 350° oven for 50 to 60 minutes or till center is almost set (it will jiggle slightly). Cool on a wire rack. Makes 8 servings.

Sun Crunchies

It's a combination of sunflower margarine, oil, and kernels that gives Ardith Zimbleman's cookie recipe lots of tasty flavor.

- 2 cups all-purpose flour
- ½ teaspoon cream of tartar
- ½ teaspoon baking soda
- ½ cup sunflower margarine
- ½ cup sugar
- ½ cup packed brown sugar
- ⅓ cup sunflower oil
- 1 egg
- ½ cup roasted, salted sunflower kernels

1. In a large bowl, combine flour, cream of tartar, and soda. In a large mixer bowl, beat together margarine, sugars, and sunflower oil with an electric mixer till smooth. Add egg and beat 3 minutes more.

2. Add the flour mixture and beat on low speed till combined. Stir in the sunflower kernels. Shape dough into 1½-inch balls and arrange on ungreased cookie sheets, or drop by rounded teaspoonfuls.

3. Bake in a 375° oven for 10 to 12 minutes. Remove cookies; cool on a wire rack. Makes 60 cookies.

Kansas may be the Sunflower State, but North Dakota grows the most domesticated sunflowers. Their sunny goodness packs these two treats, Sun Crunchies (top) and North Dakota Sunflower Pie (bottom).

Tasty Fixin's From an Ozark Kitchen

With knife in hand, Johanna Powell and her husband Walker stalk the perimeters of their homestead in Reeds Spring, not far from Branson in southwest Missouri. They're out gathering pokeweed, a spring green.

Cooking pokeweed—or similar spring greens like lamb's-quarter, curly dock, or dandelion—is a skill acquired in the Ozark hills. "I fix it the way my mother did," Johanna says. The Powells pick enough to fill Johanna's 6-quart pot, which means they need about a peck-sack's worth.

Pokeweed cooks down considerably. "The old-timers always poured bacon grease on the pokeweed or cooked it with bacon rind," Johanna says. "I just serve it with vinegar." It tastes something like a wilted spinach salad.

Citified Greens

Ozark cooks like Johanna Powell are fond of fresh, wild greens. This flavorful side dish from Sassafras! The Ozarks Cookbook *calls for garden-grown greens, available at supermarkets.*

- 4 cups water
- 1 teaspoon salt
- 1 pound fresh mustard greens or turnip greens, stemmed
  Top leaves of 6 radishes
- ½ of a small turnip, coarsely chopped (optional)
- 6 slices bacon
- 1 pound fresh spinach, stemmed
- ¼ teaspoon salt
- ¼ teaspoon fresh lemon juice
  Dash freshly ground pepper
  Dash ground nutmeg
  Sliced radishes (optional)

1. In a 5- to 6-quart Dutch oven or kettle, bring water and the 1 teaspoon salt to boiling. Add mustard or turnip greens, radish leaves, and turnip, if desired. Reduce heat and simmer, uncovered, for 30 to 45 minutes or till tender, stirring occasionally.

2. Meanwhile, in a 12-inch skillet, cook bacon till crisp. Remove bacon, reserving drippings in skillet. Drain, crumble, and set aside bacon.

3. When greens are tender, add spinach. Cover and cook for 3 to 5 minutes. Drain greens well, pressing out excess liquid. Finely chop by hand (don't use food processor).

4. Heat bacon drippings in skillet. Add greens mixture and toss to coat well. Stir in the ¼ teaspoon salt, lemon juice, pepper, nutmeg, and crumbled bacon. Sprinkle with sliced radishes, if desired, and serve immediately. Makes 4 to 6 servings.

To Use Your Microwave: Omit the 4 cups water and 1 teaspoon salt from the recipe above. Place bacon in a 3-quart casserole. Cover with paper towels. Micro-cook on 100% power (high) for 4 to 5 minutes or till done. Crumble the cooked bacon; set aside. Drain bacon drippings, reserving 2 tablespoons; set aside.

In the casserole, combine mustard greens, radish leaves, turnip, if desired, and 2 tablespoons water. Cook, covered on high for 6 minutes, stirring once. Add spinach; toss gently. Cook, covered, on high for 5 to 6 minutes or till greens are tender, stirring once. Drain and chop greens.

Add reserved bacon drippings, crumbled bacon, salt, lemon juice, pepper, and nutmeg. Toss well. Sprinkle with sliced radishes and serve immediately.

Stalking The Elusive Morel

Mushroom hunting makes for a toothsome mystery, says Michigan Judge John Voelker, author of the classic courtroom whodunit Anatomy of a Murder.

John Voelker bursts through a clump of cedars, a triumphant grin on his broad face. "Look at this beauty," he chortles, shattering the quiet in a small forest clearing in northern Michigan.

Tad Bogdan, John's long-time morel-hunting companion, casts an appreciative look as John extends his hand. In his palm lies a small mushroom, its chubby stem supporting a conical, delicately pitted brown cap. John's prize—a luscious black morel—looks like a fleshy little Christmas tree.

But it's not the morel's spongy form that draws John, Tad, and thousands of other Midwesterners to farms, acreages, and the woods each spring. It's the joy of the hunt and the morel's addictive, earthy flavor. "Hunting morels is as much fun and as challenging as fishing for brook trout," John says.

THE SCALES OF JUSTICE

John Voelker knows his fish and his fungi. The former Michigan state supreme court judge retired early to search for morels and angle for brook trout.* John won the financial freedom to pursue his life of dedicated leisure by writing the best-selling *Anatomy of a Murder* in 1957 (under the pen name Robert Traver) and later the screenplay for the film with Jimmy Stewart and Lee Remick.

These days, John writes mainly about the art of fly fishing for native—*not* stocked—brook trout. And he likes nothing better than to create an entire meal from the forest's bounty. "My ideal menu," he explains, "is black morels, native brook trout, and wild spring watercress. The watercress adds just the right tang."

Tad, a former hotel owner, restaurateur, and chef, doesn't entirely agree. "*White* morels have more flavor," he insists. Tad's wife Maggie, a long-time resident of China, often includes white morels in her home-cooked Chinese meals.

THE HEARTLAND'S GOURMET HARVEST

Whether it's black or white morels you favor, you have to find them if you want to cook them. Tinned or dried morels sell for $15 to $20 an ounce, rivaling the price of truffles and caviar. But experienced morelers

*Note: Since this feature appeared in our magazine, John Voelker has passed away. We included his story in our book as a tribute to him.

know that these shy delicacies literally do grow on—as well as under and around—trees.

Every spring, just after the last snow melts away, morel hunters—or 'shroomers, as they're known hereabouts—take to the woods across the U.S., and from France to Yugoslavia in Europe. Nowhere is the hunt as passionate as in the Midwest, where black morels spring up late in April or early in May, and white morels follow about two weeks later. Giant whites appear in June, the finale of an all-too-short season.

SEEK AND YE MIGHT FIND

Veteran 'shroomers are as secretive about their hunting grounds as California Gold Rush miners were about their claims. But they don't mind telling the sort of terrain to look for. Morels like burned-over areas, dead elms, old apple orchards, and groves of maple and ash. They sprout in sweet, loamy soil and demand just the right combination of night- and day-time temperatures.

Masters of disguise, morels are hard to spot. Concentrate! They hide among fallen leaves. Scan the ground constantly, looking from different angles to take full advantage of the light. Search up and down hillsides, especially sunny slopes.

When you spy your first morel, look for others nearby. Note the surroundings—the trees, terrain, sunlight, humidity, and ground cover. Concentrate on similar areas.

As John Voelker points out, "If it's too dry, you won't find any. If it's too wet, you won't find any, either. For me, hunting morels is a challenging mystery—eerie and fun!"

HOW TO TELL THE GOOD ONES FROM THE BAD ONES

Morels fall into two categories: "true" and "false" (morel look-alikes that can be harmful to certain people). Even if you accidentally eat a few false morels, you'll live to learn from your error. Only a few people experience any immediate reaction. Still, experts say that over time, toxins from false morels can build up in your body and cause problems. They recommend reading up on morels and making your first morel-gatherings trips with veteran hunters.

The key to identifying a true morel is to look carefully at the cap. Its entire surface must be riddled with tiny holes. The caps of false morels might be ridged, wavy, or folded, but they don't have the punched holes that distinguish true morels. The best advice: If you aren't certain about a mushroom, don't pick it.

John Voelker, left, and Tad Bogdan may disagree about whether white or black morels taste better—but they agree both are well worth the hunt.

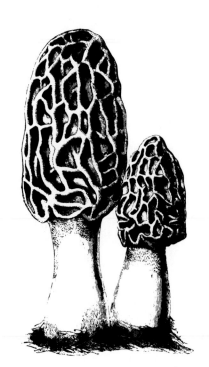

"My ideal menu," John explains, "is black morels, native brook trout, and wild spring watercress. The watercress adds just the right tang."

Chicken with Morel Cream Sauce

A hint of the woodlands makes this tender entrée unforgettable.

2 medium chicken breasts (1½
    pounds), skinned, halved
    lengthwise, and boned
¼ cup all-purpose flour
¼ teaspoon salt
¼ teaspoon dried marjoram, crushed
¼ teaspoon dried savory, crushed
⅛ teaspoon pepper
3 tablespoons butter or margarine
2 ounces fresh morels or other
    mushrooms, or ½ ounce dried
    morels, reconstituted*
2 tablespoons chopped onion
1 clove garlic, minced
1⅔ cup light cream or milk
2 tablespoons all-purpose flour
¼ teaspoon salt
1 tablespoon dry sherry
    Sprig fresh marjoram or parsley

1. Place breast halves between 2 pieces of clear plastic wrap. Pound to ¼-inch thickness; remove wrap. Combine the ¼ cup flour, ¼ teaspoon salt, marjoram, savory, and pepper. Coat chicken with flour mixture.
2. Cook chicken in butter over medium heat till done. Transfer to warm serving platter; keep warm.
3. Meanwhile, slice morels crosswise into rings. In same skillet, cook morels, onion, and garlic for 3 to 4 minutes. In a small bowl, combine cream or milk, the 2 tablespoons flour, and ¼ teaspoon salt; add to vegetables in skillet. Cook and stir till thickened and bubbly; add sherry. Cook and stir for 1 minute.
4. Spoon some sauce over chicken; pass remainder. Garnish chicken with fresh marjoram or parsley. Serves 4.
Note: To reconstitute mushrooms, cover morels with warm water. Let stand for 45 minutes; drain.

Morel-Zucchini Frittata

A generous sprinkling of morels dresses up this Italian cousin of the omelet.

4 ounces fresh morels or other
    mushrooms, or 1 ounce dried
    morels, reconstituted (see
    note, left)
½ cup chopped zucchini
1 tablespoon chopped onion
1 tablespoon chopped green pepper
2 tablespoons butter or margarine
6 eggs
¼ cup milk
¼ teaspoon salt
    Dash pepper
    Tomato wedges
    Parsley sprigs

1. In a 10-inch ovenproof skillet, cook morels (cut large ones into bite-size strips), zucchini, onion, and green pepper in butter or margarine till zucchini is tender and most of the liquid has evaporated.
2. In a mixing bowl, beat eggs with milk, salt, and pepper; pour over vegetable mixture in skillet. Cook over medium-low heat, lifting edges occasionally. Cook about 4 minutes or till edges begin to set and the underside is lightly browned.
3. Place pan under broiler, 4 to 5 inches from heat. Broil about 2 minutes or just till set. Loosen sides and bottom of frittata with a spatula. Serve immediately from skillet or slide frittata, faceup, onto a warm serving platter. Garnish with tomato wedges and parsley. Makes 3 servings.

Shops

Come with us on a Midwest shopping spree. We'll skip right by the bustling shopping malls and trendy boutiques and head straight for the true treasures of the Heartland—the food shops. On our trip we'll visit Missouri, Nebraska, Kansas, Minnesota, Michigan, Wisconsin, Iowa, and Ohio. For feather-light pastries, crusty breads, and fresh-from-the-oven cookies, we'll stop at four bakeries. Next, we'll track down Heartland sausage makers and sample their plump, savory wursts. Just for the fun of it, we'll investigate the nooks and crannies of three old-time mills and stock up on the wholesome grain products they produce. Then, we'll give in to our sweet tooths and find three great spots to buy candies of all kinds—everything from buttery caramels to bittersweet truffles. What's more, we'll collect recipes from our food-shop pros, so you can make all of these great foods at home.

Best of the Wursts

From ballpark bratwursts to pizzas smothered in pepperoni,

Midwesterners love their sausage. And the region's sausage makers

lovingly reciprocate with a hearty array of traditional favorites with

names like bockwurst, jaternice, and potatoskorv—links to a proud

immigrant past. Meet three masters of the grinder, and sample their

top sausage recipes.

Woods'

Edward Woods has made a career of spicing up the sausage scene in Bowling Green, Missouri.

"I detest anything bland," confesses Ed Woods, a burly, mustached man who also answers to "Sweet Betsy." The nickname? Sunbonneted "Sweet Betsy from Pike" of folk-song fame adorns the logo of Woods Smoked Meats, the business that Ed inherited from his father more than a decade ago.

You can bet a good Missouri mule that Betsy's renowned sausages, hams, and slow-smoked bacon aren't bland. Ed's robust Italian sausage is a particular favorite of the spice-loving set that frequents his shop, 30 miles south of Hannibal in northeast Missouri. The sausage is based on a recipe from Ed's wife Regina, who once owned an Italian restaurant.

Ed's office is down-home and informal. Old freezer lockers serve as file cabinets. A massive roll-top desk bears the inscription, "Last chew, third day of April, 1915," the legacy of a reformed tobacco user. But Ed isn't casual about his products.

A graduate of the University of Missouri, with a degree in food science and nutrition, Ed is a stickler for quality and flavor. "We use the best, leanest meats available. And we use only natural spices." Betsy's sausages win awards year after year, and the sugar-cured bacon claims a half dozen grand prizes from the American Association of Meat Processors.

Ed is an astute, hard-driving businessman with a flair for marketing and managing his thriving mail-order trade. The payoff for all the hard work is watching satisfied looks on customers' faces as they bite into Betsy's meats. "They can't get enough," says Ed.

Woods Smoked Meats, Highway 54W, Bowling Green, MO 63334.

Sausage Soufflé

Ed Woods' no-fail soufflé is really a strata casserole in disguise.

1½ pounds bulk Italian sausage
 6 slices white bread
 1 cup shredded mozzarella cheese
 4 eggs
 2 cups milk
 ½ teaspoon salt
 ½ teaspoon dry mustard

1. In a large skillet, cook Italian sausage till brown. Drain off fat. Cut the crusts from the bread slices, if desired. Cut bread into cubes.
2. In a 12x7½x2-inch baking dish, evenly spread *half* of the sausage. Top with bread cubes, then shredded mozzarella cheese. Sprinkle with remaining sausage.
3. In a mixing bowl combine eggs, milk, salt, and mustard. Pour into baking dish. Cover and refrigerate for 3 to 24 hours.
4. To serve, bake, covered, in a 325° oven for 30 minutes. Uncover; bake for 15 to 20 minutes more or till a knife inserted near the center comes out clean. Let stand for 10 minutes. Makes 8 servings.

Stoysich's

Rudy, Norman, Rita, and Ken Stoysich are Omaha's reigning family of old-style sausage makers.

"Look at this," commands Rudy Stoysich, hefting a dictionary-thick book and pointing out its gold-lettered title: *Everything I Know About Sausage Making* by Rudy Stoysich. Rudy savors the compliments on his vast knowledge. Then, he opens the book for his impressed guest and fans the contents—about 1,500 blank pages.

Rudy chuckles. Actually, he *could* fill a lot of those pages with what he's learned during a long career of blending spices and feeding the grinder. But Omaha's premier sausage maker isn't about to reveal the recipes for his prizewinning products—from bockwurst to jaternice to chorizo and salami, more than 100 varieties.

However, Rudy *is* confiding everything he knows to sons Ken and Norman, who soon will take over the business when their father retires. Norman oversees a satellite store in suburban west Omaha; Rudy, his wife Rita, and red-bearded Ken work in the original south Omaha store.

Some of the best recipes Norman and Ken have learned were entrusted to Rudy by customers. "People want me to make sausage like their parents made," he explains. "So, they share their recipes."

Over the last quarter century, Stoysich's has evolved from a little corner grocery, serving Omaha's tight-knit Polish and Czech neighborhoods (Rudy is of Hungarian descent), into an upscale butcher shop frequented by meat and sausage gourmets from throughout Nebraska and neighboring states. Rudy keeps his loyal customers happy by offering the latest in trendy spiral-cut hams, range chickens, and swordfish steaks. But sausage is still the main draw. After all, Rudy wrote the book.

Stoysich House of Sausage, 2532 S. 24th St., Omaha, NE 68108 (402/341-7260). No mail orders.

Stoysich's has evolved from a little corner grocery into an upscale butcher shop frequented by gourmets from throughout Nebraska and neighboring states. Sausage is still the main draw.

Rotini-Pepperoni Salad

Halve Rita Stoysich's recipe for this potluck-size salad to serve a smaller crowd. Rita says it's great with steak.

1	16-ounce box *rotini* or *large elbow macaroni*
¾	cup *salad oil*
⅓	cup *lemon juice*
1	tablespoon *sugar*
1½	teaspoons *dried basil, crushed*
½	teaspoon *dried oregano, crushed*
½	teaspoon *crushed red pepper*
½	teaspoon *salt*
¼	teaspoon *garlic powder*
¼	teaspoon *pepper*
1	16-ounce can *stewed tomatoes*
1½	cups *chopped green pepper*
1	cup *sliced green onions*
½	cup *sliced pitted ripe olives*
1	4-ounce package *sliced pepperoni, halved*

1. In a saucepan, cook rotini or elbow macaroni according to package directions. Drain.

2. Meanwhile, for dressing, in a screw-top jar, combine salad oil, lemon juice, sugar, basil, oregano, red pepper, salt, garlic powder, and pepper. Cover and shake well.

3. In a large bowl, combine the rotini, tomatoes, green pepper, green onions, olives, and pepperoni. Drizzle the dressing over salad mixture; toss to coat. Cover and chill for 4 to 24 hours. Makes 10 to 12 servings.

Roepke's

LueAnn, Brad, and Al Roepke are the links to superior sausage in Waterville, Kansas.

Roepke bologna and summer sausage are cherished by the descendants of the Germans, Bohemians, and Swedes who settled the farmlands surrounding this Kansas town.

"We ate an awful lot of mistakes," says Al Roepke, recalling when he and his father-in-law Chris Herrmann taught themselves to make sausage using the time-honored method of trial and error. Their back-room seminars in spices, grinding, and stuffing began in 1956, when Al returned to the northeast Kansas farm town to find that Chris had bought a meat processing and locker plant. "I needed a job," says Al, "and he had one to offer."

Fortunately, they learned their lessons well. Al and his wife LueAnn bought out Chris more than 20 years ago, and these days, Roepke bologna and summer sausage are cherished by the descendants of the Germans, Bohemians, and Swedes who settled the rolling farmland hereabouts. Al and LueAnn oversee the busy meat counter and newly installed delicatessen. Son Brad manages the meat processing plant.

It was by chance that the family gained the recipe for its best known sausage, potatoskorv—delicately delicious, Swedish-style links stuffed with a lightly spiced grind of potatoes and pork. When nearby Tuttle Creek Reservoir was filled in the 1960s, the village of Randolph ended up at the bottom. One of its citizens, who migrated a few miles north to Waterville, dropped by Roepke's to offer her special recipe for potatoskorv. "A lot of people like it," she bragged. She was right. These days, the Roepkes sell tons of potatoskorv, especially at Christmas.

Al says that hardly a week passes without someone walking into the shop clutching a sausage recipe touted as a surefire winner. Al doesn't encourage those folks. But every once in awhile, he'll try out one of the recipes . . . you never know.

Roepke Processing Plant, 411 E. Main St., Waterville, KS 66548 (913/785-2558). No mail orders.

Sausage and Mostaccioli Bake

To accompany this hearty main dish, LueAnn Roepke tosses together an apple, spinach, and raisin salad.

8	ounces mostaccioli, rigatoni, or rotelle (3½ cups)
1½	pounds bulk pork sausage
½	cup chopped onion
¼	cup chopped green pepper
1	clove garlic, minced
1	16-ounce can tomatoes, cut up
1	6-ounce can tomato paste
½	cup water
¼	teaspoon dried oregano, crushed
⅛	teaspoon pepper
6	ounces shredded American cheese (1½ cups)

1. In a saucepan, cook pasta according to package directions. Drain.
2. Meanwhile, in a 12-inch skillet, cook sausage, onion, green pepper, and garlic till meat is brown and onion is tender. Drain off fat.
3. Stir the *undrained* tomatoes, tomato paste, water, oregano, and pepper into the mixture in skillet. Stir in the cooked pasta.
4. Spoon *half* of the mostaccioli mixture into a 3-quart casserole. Sprinkle with *half* of the cheese. Top with the remaining mostaccioli mixture.
5. Bake in a 350° oven for 35 minutes. Sprinkle with the remaining cheese. Bake about 5 minutes more or till cheese melts. Makes 8 servings.

Sausage-Mushroom Strudel

Rita Stoysich serves this for dinner with a vegetable salad.

- 1 pound sweet Italian sausage
- 1 pound fresh mushrooms, finely chopped
- ¼ cup finely chopped shallots or green onions
- 1 8-ounce package cream cheese, softened
- 8 18x12-inch sheets phyllo dough
- ½ cup butter or margarine, melted
- 2 tablespoons dry bread crumbs

  Green onion tops, cut into brushes (optional)
  Halved whole fresh mushroom (optional)

1. In a 12-inch skillet, cook sausage, chopped mushrooms, and shallots or green onions over medium-high heat about 8 minutes or till sausage is no longer pink, stirring occasionally. Drain. Stir in cream cheese. Set aside.
2. On a damp dish towel or 24-inch length of waxed paper, arrange a sheet of phyllo dough. Brush with some melted butter or margarine and sprinkle with a scant 1 teaspoon bread crumbs. Repeat with 6 more sheets of phyllo dough, placing them on top of the first sheet. Place the last sheet of phyllo dough on top. Brush with butter or margarine.
3. Leaving a 2-inch border, spoon sausage mixture along a narrow side of dough. Using cloth or waxed paper as a guide, roll up. Tuck ends under.
4. Place strudel, seam side down, in a shallow baking pan. Brush the strudel with the remaining melted butter or margarine. Bake in a 400° oven about 20 minutes or till golden brown. Garnish the strudel with onion brushes and mushroom halves, if desired. Makes 6 main-dish servings.

German Skillet Supper

Ed Woods says this cabbage-and-sausage skillet dinner is his favorite meal (we added the microwave variation).

- 6 slices bacon
- 1 medium head cabbage, cored and cut into 6 wedges
- 1 medium onion, chopped
- ¼ cup water
- 2 tablespoons sugar
- 1 clove garlic, minced
- 2 teaspoons caraway seed
- 1 pound fully cooked Polish kielbasa, cut into 6 pieces

1. In a large skillet, cook bacon till crisp. Remove and drain on paper towels. Reserve 2 tablespoons of the bacon drippings in the skillet.
2. To the skillet, add cabbage wedges, onion, water, sugar, garlic, and caraway seed. Bring to boiling; reduce heat. Cover and cook over medium-low heat for 10 minutes.
3. Add Polish kielbasa to skillet. Cover and cook for 5 to 10 minutes more or till cabbage is tender and sausage is heated through. Crumble bacon and sprinkle over the cabbage mixture. Makes 4 to 6 servings.
To Use Your Microwave: In a microwave-safe, 3-quart casserole or 8x8x2-inch baking dish, micro-cook bacon, covered, on 100% power (high) for 6 to 8 minutes or till done. Remove and drain on paper towels. Reserve 2 tablespoons of the bacon drippings in the casserole.

To the casserole, add cabbage, onion, water, sugar, garlic, and caraway seed. Cover and cook on high about 10 minutes or till the cabbage is almost tender, rearranging cabbage once. Add Polish kielbasa and cook for 5 to 8 minutes more or till cabbage is tender and sausage is heated through. Serve as above.

Sausage-Wild Rice Casserole

LueAnn Roepke adds leftover turkey from Thanksgiving or Christmas to this main dish.

- 12 ounces mild pork sausage
- 1 cup chopped onion
- 8 ounces sliced fresh mushrooms
- 1 8-ounce can sliced water chestnuts, drained
- ¼ cup all-purpose flour
- ⅛ teaspoon pepper
- 1½ cups chicken broth
- ¾ cup milk
- 1 6¼- or 6½-ounce package quick-cooking long grain and wild rice mix
- 2 cups cubed, cooked chicken or turkey

1. In a 12-inch skillet, cook sausage and onion till sausage is brown. Drain off fat. Add sliced mushrooms and water chestnuts and cook till mushrooms are tender. Stir in flour and pepper. Add chicken broth and milk all at once. Cook and stir till mixture is thickened and bubbly. Cook and stir for 1 minute more. Remove skillet from heat.
2. Meanwhile, in a saucepan, cook long grain and wild rice mix according to package directions.
3. Toss together the sausage mixture, rice, and chicken or turkey. Transfer to a 2½- or 3-quart casserole.
4. Bake, uncovered, in a 350° oven for 25 to 30 minutes or till heated through. Makes 6 servings.

Pictured clockwise from left: Sausage-Mushroom Strudel, Sausage-Wild Rice Casserole, and German Skillet Supper.

Baker's Choice

Irresistible Christmas creations roll from the ovens of scores of bakers across the Midwest who celebrate their ethnic heritage. Their yuletide treats, featured on the pages that follow, are sure to become holiday baking traditions at your house.

Tattered, flour-smudged, yellowed pages of two loose-leaf notebooks hold Jerabek Bakery's secrets. After his father Ed opened the bakery in 1905, Ed Jerabek, Jr., jotted down the recipes, which translate into scrumptious German-Bohemian cookies, cakes, tarts, and crusty breads.

"We bake the old favorites that customers come back for," smiles Mellissa Zerwas, step-granddaughter of Ed, Jr., and a fourth-generation baker. She and her parents Dieta and Will Deyo, along with Mellissa's baker-husband Darrell, keep Jerabek's a family operation.

When Ed, Jr.'s, Bohemian father married his German wife Hildegard, the bakery's treats got a German touch. Though Ed died in 1975, Hildegard still stops by regularly to visit.

During the fall, before the holidays, flour flies 23 hours a day, and Mellissa's three brothers join

Jerabek Bakery

ST. PAUL, MINNESOTA

the bakery crew. "We start with peanut brittle and fruitcakes," says Mellissa. Then, it's on to the fun Christmas breads, like braided German stollen. "We have a hard time keeping up with the cookies especially," chuckles Will. "As fast as we bake them, they go out the door."

Jerabek Bakery, 61 W. Winifred St., St. Paul MN 55107.

Cookie Hint

To get as many cookies from your cookie dough as possible, leave as little space between cutouts as you can. Then combine the scraps, being sure to handle the dough lightly to keep the cookies tender. Reroll the dough on a floured surface and cut additional cookies.

Jerabek's Cheese Tarts

Dieta Deyo's grandmother Eichhols first made these German holiday tarts.

2 cups all-purpose flour
1 cup butter
1 cup small-curd cottage cheese
  Desired jam, preserves, or
    marmalade
  Powdered Sugar Icing

1. In a large mixing bowl, cut together the flour, butter, and cottage cheese till mixture clings together. Form the mixture into a ball.
2. On a floured surface, roll out dough to form a 12x10-inch rectangle. Starting with a short end, fold in half. Repeat, rolling out and folding dough 4 more times.
3. Roll out dough to form a 15x11-inch rectangle. Using a diamond-shaped cutter (about 3½x2½ inches), cut out cookies and place on lightly greased cookie sheets. Press an indentation in each, then spoon in ¼ *teaspoon* jam, preserves, or marmalade.
4. Bake in a 400° oven about 15 minutes or till golden brown. Remove from cookie sheets and cool on wire racks. Drizzle with Powdered Sugar Icing. Makes 36 cookies.
Powdered Sugar Icing: In a small mixing bowl, combine 1 cup sifted *powdered sugar* and 1 to 2 tablespoons *water*.

Ed Jerabek, Jr., and staff show off some of their tempting offerings.

Jerabek's Linzer Cookies

Bakery devotees return again and again during the holidays to buy these crisp German cookies by the dozens.

2 cups sifted cake flour
1¾ cups crushed vanilla wafers or white
    cake crumbs
1 cup ground hazelnuts (filberts)
1 cup sugar
¼ cup shortening
¼ cup butter
2 eggs
¼ teaspoon ground cinnamon
¼ teaspoon ground cloves
¼ teaspoon ground allspice

⅛ teaspoon salt
  Red and green candied-cherry pieces,
    slivered almonds, and/or
    hazelnut halves*

1. Lightly grease cookie sheets or line them with parchment paper. In a mixing bowl, stir together the cake flour, crushed vanilla wafers or white cake crumbs, and ground hazelnuts. Set the flour mixture aside.
2. In a large mixing bowl, beat sugar, shortening, and butter with an electric mixer till fluffy. Add the eggs, cinnamon, cloves, allspice, and salt; beat till well mixed. Add flour mixture and mix well. (The dough should be sticky, not stiff. If cake crumbs are quite moist, stir in ¼ cup additional sifted cake flour. If the dough is too sticky to roll out, cover and chill it thoroughly before working with it.)
3. On a lightly floured surface, roll the cookie dough to ⅛-inch thickness. Use decorative cookie cutters to cut out the rolled dough. Transfer the cutout cookies to the prepared cookie sheets. Decorate with red and green candied cherries, slivered almonds, and/or hazelnut halves.
4. Bake the cookies in a 350° oven for 10 to 12 minutes or till firm and the edges are just golden. Remove from cookie sheets and cool on wire racks. Makes about 60 cookies.
Note: It's easier to halve hazelnuts if you blanch them first in boiling water.

O&H Kleiners

Jerabek's Linzer Cookies

...'s Cheese Tarts

O&H Kringle

Dutch Delite Banket

Dutch Delite Krakeling

Sykora's Vaňočka

Dutch Delite Pastry Shoppe

The drone of a four-wheel drive cracks the crisp night air, as it rolls across the snow in Holland, Michigan. It's just midnight when Ralph Van Asperen flicks on the light at his Dutch Delite Pastry Shoppe. Then, the mixing and kneading begins.

Ralph has logged more than 35 years in the baking business. At age 12, he stood on a bread box to reach a table in his family's bakery in the Netherlands. Ralph remembers his father delivering baked goods by canal boat then.

Ralph is taller now. And in his cozy, 20-seat coffee shop—papered in delft blue—customers linger over coffee and pastries as they watch Ralph in the adjoining kitchen.

At Christmas, they're likely to see him turning out his treats at a frantic pace. Speed is essential when making Dutch cookies called krakeling; the buttery dough can melt.

"You have to fly," grins this mountain of a man with a mockingly gruff manner and the heart of a teddy bear. "It's a tough cookie to make."

Does Ralph, who has a college degree in accounting, ever tire of his baked goods? He jokes, "At quitting time, I've got to have coffee and something sweet to eat on the way home—that's a nine-minute ride. And I still sing on my way to work."

Dutch Delite Pastry Shoppe, 45 E. Eighth St., Holland, MI 49423.

Dutch Delite Butterdough

This dough is the basis for several of Ralph Van Asperen's recipes. You can watch him make it at his bakery in Holland, Michigan. Ralph knocked out the wall between his kitchen and coffee shop so he can greet customers who come in while he's working.

1 pound butter (2 cups), chilled (do not use margarine)
4 cups all-purpose flour
1 cup water

1. Coarsely chop the butter. In a large mixing bowl, combine the butter, flour, and water. (Flour will not be completely moistened.)

2. On a lightly floured surface, knead the dough 10 times, pressing and pushing the pieces of dough together to form a rough ball. (The dough still will have some areas that look dry and some chunks of the butter will be visible.)

3. Turn the dough out onto a well-floured surface. Roll out the dough to form a 17x12-inch rectangle. Fold ⅓ of the dough over the center third and fold the remaining third over the top (creating three layers). Cover the dough with a clean dish towel or waxed paper and let rest for 5 minutes in the refrigerator.

4. Repeat Step 3. Let rest, covered, for 10 minutes more in the refrigerator. Repeat, rolling and folding into the 3 layers. Wrap the dough in plastic wrap. Chill the dough overnight in the refrigerator. Makes enough dough for 2 batches of Krakeling or 2 batches of Bankets.

Dutch Delite Bankets

Ralph Van Asperen's 80-plus-year-old mom is a good customer for these pastries.

- 1   beaten egg
- 1   8-ounce can almond paste
- 1   cup sugar
- 3   tablespoons all-purpose flour
- ½   recipe chilled Dutch Delite
  Butterdough (see recipe,
  opposite)
  Icing
  Purchased decorator icing

1. Reserve *1 tablespoon* of the beaten egg; set aside. In a mixing bowl, beat together the remaining egg, almond paste, sugar, and flour till blended. Divide mixture in half. Shape each half into a 13-inch-long roll.
2. Roll out Butterdough to form a 14-inch square. Cut in half, forming two 14x7-inch rectangles. Place 1 of the almond-paste rolls on 1 rectangle of dough, positioned close to a long side of dough, leaving about ½ inch of dough at top and bottom of almond roll. Beginning at that long side, roll up dough, jelly-roll style, with the almond paste inside.
3. Transfer pastry to an ungreased baking sheet. Shape into a circle, joining ends; seal. Brush with reserved egg. Repeat with the remaining almond-paste roll and dough rectangle.
4. Bake in a 375° oven for 30 to 35 minutes or till golden brown. Transfer to wire racks; cool. Ice and decorate pastry rings as desired. Makes 2 pastries (16 to 20 servings).
Icing: In a bowl, combine 1 cup sifted *powdered sugar* and 1 to 2 tablespoons *water or milk.*

Dutch Delite Banket

Dutch Delite Krakeling

At Ralph Van Asperen's bakery, many of the recipes—like the one for these crispy figure-8 cookies—came from Ralph's father, originally a baker in the Netherlands. The cookies are as authentically Dutch as the town's windmill, which spins round in the chilling winter breeze.

- ½   recipe chilled Dutch Delite
  Butterdough (see recipe,
  opposite)
  Sugar

1. On floured surface, roll Butterdough into a 14x8-inch rectangle.
2. Cut dough lengthwise into two 14x4-inch strips. Cut each of these strips crosswise into ½-inch strips, making fifty-six 4x½-inch strips total. (To make a larger cookie, roll dough into a 12x9-inch rectangle. Cut the dough crosswise into two 9x6-inch strips. Then, cut the dough crosswise into ½-inch strips, making thirty-six 6x½-inch strips total.)
3. Generously sprinkle a piece of waxed paper with some sugar. Shape strips into figure 8s. Place, several at a time, on the sugar, leaving space between each figure 8. Sprinkle generously with more sugar. Using a rolling pin, roll figure 8s till they're about 3 inches long and ¹/₁₆-inch thick. (If you're making the larger cookies, roll them till they're about 4½ inches long and ¹/₁₆-inch thick.)
4. Place 1 inch apart on an ungreased cookie sheet. Bake in a 350° oven for 16 to 18 minutes or till golden brown. Remove from cookie sheets and cool on wire racks. Makes 56 small or 36 large cookies.

A heady wave of mouth-watering aromas greets customers at the O&H Danish Bakery. Pay attention, and you probably can distinguish the baked brown sugar, cinnamon, and pecans—just a few of the ingredients in this bakery's specialty: kringle.

Eric, Dale, and Mike Olesen, along with their parents Ray and Myrna, produce more kringle than any of the seven other bakeries in Racine, self-proclaimed kringle capital of the nation. The Olesens ship up to 60,000 kringle all over the world during December. They sell thousands more to walk-in customers. In fact, the family will tell you about folks who rush to Racine to buy their O&H Kringle between flights at Chicago's O'Hare airport.

The Olesen brothers' grandfather, a native of Aalborg, Denmark, started the O&H Kringle tradition (he still stops in to check on the business). But the new generation of Olesens now calls the shots. At the height of production, the bakery turns out upwards of 500 kringle an hour. Myrna is the resident quality-control expert. "I'm the best customer and the best critic," she smiles.

You can make O&H Kringle and Kleiners at home or order kringle by mail from: *O & H Danish Bakery, 1841 Douglas Ave., Racine, WI 53402 (800/227-6665).*

RACINE, WISCONSIN
O&H Danish Bakery

O&H Kleiners
This sweet Danish pastry is a cross between a cookie and a doughnut.

3¾ cups sifted cake flour or 3 cups
    unsifted all-purpose flour
1 teaspooon baking powder
½ teaspoon ground cardamom
¼ teaspoon salt
3 egg yolks
1 egg
1 cup sugar
2 tablespoons butter, softened
¼ cup milk
    Cooking oil for deep-fat frying
    Powdered sugar (optional)

1. In a mixing bowl, stir together flour, baking powder, cardamom, and salt; set aside.
2. In a large mixing bowl, beat egg yolks and whole egg slightly with an electric mixer. Add the sugar and beat on high speed for 2 to 3 minutes or till light colored. Beat in the softened butter.
3. Add the flour mixture and the milk alternately to the egg mixture, beating after each addition just till blended. (Stir in the last portion of the flour mixture by hand.)
4. On a lightly floured surface, roll the dough into an ⅛-inch-thick

rectangle. Make lengthwise parallel cuts 2 inches apart in the dough. Then make diagonal cuts, at a 45° angle to the first cuts and about 2 inches apart, to form diamonds. Reroll the dough scraps and repeat.

5. In each diamond, cut a 1½-inch lengthwise slit in the center. Gently push 1 long point of the dough through slit, then gently pull point back to same end (see photo, page 85).

6. Fry 3 or 4 pastries at a time in deep, hot oil (365°) about 1½ minutes or till golden brown, turning once. Drain on paper towels. Sprinkle with powdered sugar, if desired. Makes about 48 pastries.

Note: Kleiners are best when they're served the same day as made. Or pack them in freezer containers; seal, label, and freeze for up to 1 month. If you freeze Kleiners, dust them with powdered sugar after thawing.

O&H Kringle
Sixteen folds of flaky dough layered with butter, a brown sugar filling, and pecans.

    ¾ cup butter, softened
    1 package active dry yeast
    ¼ cup warm water (105° to 115°)
    ¼ cup sugar
    ¼ cup warm milk (105° to 115°)
    1 egg
    ½ teaspoon salt
    ½ teaspoon lemon extract
    2 cups all-purpose flour
       Butterscotch Filling
    1 cup chopped pecans
       Powdered Sugar Icing

1. Halve the butter. On each of 2 pieces of waxed paper, spread 1 portion of butter to form an 8-inch square. Wrap and chill the butter portions.

2. In a mixing bowl, soften the yeast in warm water. Add sugar, warm milk, egg, salt, and lemon extract; mix well. Add 1¾ *cups* of the flour and beat till mixture forms a ball. Turn out onto a floured surface. Knead in the remaining flour till dough is smooth and elastic (2 to 3 minutes total). Cover and let rest for 5 minutes.

3. Roll out the dough to form a 12x8-inch rectangle. Place 1 square of chilled butter on ⅔ of a dough rectangle next to an 8-inch side. Fold uncovered ⅓ of dough over middle third. Then, fold opposite third over the top.

4. Next, from a 4-inch end of the rectangle, fold dough over middle third and fold opposite 4-inch end over the top, making a stack of layered dough. Cover and refrigerate the stacked dough for 30 minutes.

5. Repeat, rolling dough into a 12x8-inch rectangle. Top with remaining square of butter; fold into a stack as above. Cover and refrigerate 2 hours.

6. Prepare the Butterscotch Filling.

7. Cut the chilled dough in half; chill 1 portion. On a floured surface, roll out the remaining portion of dough, smooth side up, to form a 24x6-inch rectangle. (If dough is too elastic and hard to roll, cover and let rest for 5 to 10 minutes.) Spread *half* of the Butterscotch Filling lengthwise down center third of dough. Sprinkle with *half* of the pecans. Fold 1 of the 24-inch-long sides over filling; brush other side with *water* and fold over the top. Pinch the dough to seal well.

8. Transfer the filled dough to a greased baking sheet and shape into an oval. Seal ends together. Flatten dough slightly with hands. Repeat shaping with remaining dough. Cover the ovals of dough and let rise till a slight indentation remains in the dough when touched (about 1 hour).

9. Bake in a 350° oven for 20 to 25 minutes or till golden brown. Remove from baking sheets and cool on wire racks. Drizzle with icing while warm. Makes 2 filled ovals.

Butterscotch Filling: In a mixing bowl, stir together 1 cup packed *brown sugar*, dash *salt*, and dash ground *cinnamon*. Cut in ⅓ cup *butter*. Add 1 *egg white* and mix well.

Powdered Sugar Icing: In a mixing bowl, beat together 1 cup sifted *powdered sugar* and 1 to 2 tablespoons *water*.

O&H Kringle

Sykora Bakery

"**I** worked nights for 40 years. That's enough," laughs Les Sykora. Now that he's over 70 years old and "sort of semiretired," Les admits that he sometimes doesn't slip on his apron till nearly 6:30 a.m. By then, the night crew at Les' Cedar Rapids, Iowa, bakery has been working for hours.

During the holidays, Les works his squat Hubbard-brand oven (patented 1888) overtime, as faithful customers flock to the city's Czech Village to stock up at the Sykora Bakery. Les' braided sweet bread is a favorite.

Les learned the art of baking at the elbow of his father Joseph, who immigrated to the U.S. from what was then Bohemia. The elder Sykora moved his family into the bakery's upstairs apartment in 1927, after buying the business from his boss—and marrying the boss' Bohemian cleaning girl. A wedding portrait of Les' parents still hangs in the bakery.

Bragging that he's "100 percent" Czech, Les happily dons his Czech costume for special occasions. The chalet-style shop is a showplace for Les' zany collection of memorabilia donated by customers, including "Bohemian binoculars" (beer bottles taped together) and a sign: "We accept all out of town Czechs."

Sykora Bakery, 73 16th Ave. SW, Cedar Rapids, IA 52404.

Sykora's Vaňočka

"The name of this bread comes from the word Van-oce in Czech, which means Christmas," explains Les Sykora. Braid the dough carefully, and it will hold its shape while baking. Les sometimes frosts the loaf.

- 1 package active dry yeast
- ¼ cup warm water (105° to 115°)
- ½ cup sugar
- ¼ cup margarine or butter
- 2 teaspoons salt
- 2 eggs
- 5½ to 6 cups all-purpose flour
- 1 cup warm milk (105° to 115°)
- 1 teaspoon finely shredded lemon peel
- ¼ teaspoon ground mace
- 1 cup light raisins
- ½ cup chopped nuts
- 1 beaten egg yolk

1. Soften yeast in warm water. In a mixing bowl, beat together sugar, margarine or butter, and salt. Add eggs; beat well. Beat in *1 cup* of the flour. Beat in milk, lemon peel, mace, and yeast mixture. Stir in as much remaining flour as you can with a spoon. Stir in raisins and nuts.

2. Turn out onto a floured surface. Knead in enough of the remaining flour to make a moderately soft dough that is smooth and elastic (3 to 5 minutes total). Place in a lightly greased bowl; turn once to grease surface. Cover; let rise in a warm place till doubled (about 1½ hours).

3. Punch the dough down; divide in half. Divide 1 portion of dough into fourths for the bottom braid; cover and let rest for 10 minutes.

Meanwhile, divide remaining bread dough into 5 portions for the other 2 layers of the dough. Cover those portions and set aside.

4. On a lightly floured surface, form each of the first 4 portions into a 16-inch-long rope. On a greased baking sheet, arrange the 4 ropes 1 inch apart. Beginning in the middle of the ropes, braid loosely together toward each end. (To braid 4 ropes, overlap the center 2 ropes to form an X. Take the outside left rope and cross over the closest middle rope. Then, take the outside right rope and cross under the closest middle rope. Repeat braiding until you reach the end.) Pinch ends together; tuck under. Turn baking sheet and braid on opposite end. Gently pull width of braid out slightly.

5. Form remaining 5 portions into 16-inch-long ropes. Braid 3 of the ropes together. Brush the 4-strand braid with *water* and center the second braid on top; gently pull width of top braid out slightly.

6. Twist the remaining 2 strands of dough together. Brush the top braid with *water*; place the twist on top of the second braid. Cover the shaped dough and let rise till nearly double.

7. Brush surface of the shaped dough with beaten egg yolk. Bake in a 350° oven for 35 to 40 minutes or till golden brown. Cover the loaf with foil during the last 10 minutes of baking. Remove from baking sheet; cool on a wire rack. Makes 1 braid (16 servings).

Czech Christmas treats created by Les Sykora of the Sykora Bakery.

Stone-Ground Goodness

The sounds of millstones, waterwheels, and streams have echoed across the Heartland for generations. Join us on visits to three surviving mills, where you can still hear those serenades and sample favorite treats of millers who grind the grains.

Skillful millers know how to coax the best grinds of specialty flours, meals, and mixes for devoted customers.

The Frankenmuth Mill's real job is to provide visitors with a peek at history. Signs throughout the mill describe the machinery and operation for those taking self-guided tours.

Frankenmuth Mill has had its share of ups and downs. Built in 1848 to serve the German immigrants settling east-central Michigan, the Hubinger Mill, as it was known originally, burned to the ground in 1911, was rebuilt, and milled Frankenmuth's grain four more decades before falling into disrepair and being torn down in the 1950's.

But folks here missed the old mill. In 1981, they collected money, gathered the know-how, and painstakingly resurrected the mill from scratch. Its waterwheel has been spinning in the Cass River's steady current ever since.

"Our new mill is a glorified version of what it used to be," says Gerald Braun, manager. "If you'd come here 80 years ago, you'd have seen the same machinery."

All the interior parts of the proud, 3½-story wooden structure—right down to the grinding stones—were salvaged from other old mills. Of course, everything works. Water jetting across wooden paddles spins the 13-foot-in-diameter waterwheel, rotating a heavy central shaft. The shaft, in turn, transfers its relentless power to iron gears. Those gears spin smaller shafts that rotate thick

continued

Quick-Fix Corn Sticks

This Frankenmuth Mill quick bread makes owning a corn-stick mold worthwhile. But you also can bake muffins with part or all of the batter.

---

  1 cup cornmeal
  1 cup all-purpose flour
 ⅓ cup sugar
  4 teaspoons baking powder
 ½ teaspoon salt
  1 beaten egg
  1 cup milk
 ¼ cup shortening, melted

1. Grease corn-stick pans*. Heat in a 425° oven. For muffins, grease muffin pans or line with paper bake cups.
2. In a large mixing bowl, stir together cornmeal, flour, sugar, baking powder, and salt. In a small bowl, combine egg, milk, and melted shortening. Add to dry ingredients all at once and stir just till flour is moistened; batter should still be lumpy.
3. Fill hot corn-stick pans ⅔ full with batter; bake in a 425° oven for 10 to 12 minutes. Or, fill muffin pans ⅔ full; bake for 15 to 18 minutes. Makes 18 to 20 corn sticks or 12 muffins.
Note: If you wish to make corn sticks with all the batter and have just 1 corn-stick pan, bake several batches. The batter will hold while it waits to be baked.

A TOWN RECLAIMS ITS MILL

Frankenmuth

"Grinding coarse cornmeal is tidy business, compared to milling powdery wheat flour," says Gerald.

Bavarian Honey-Bran Muffins

Moist, hot breads, originally baked in Frankenmuth's Bavarian Inn restaurant.

---

   2 cups natural wheat bran (white
       wheat bran)
   2 cups all-purpose flour
  ¾ cup raisins
  ¼ cup sugar
1¼ teaspoons baking soda
  ¼ teaspoon salt
   1 beaten egg
  ¾ cup milk
  ⅔ cup honey
  ½ cup margarine, melted

1. In a large bowl, stir together wheat bran, flour, raisins, sugar, baking soda, and salt. In a small bowl, combine egg, milk, honey, and melted margarine. Add all at once to flour mixture. Stir just till moistened; don't beat.

2. Grease muffin cups or line with paper bake cups; fill ⅔ full. Bake in a 400° oven for 16 to 18 minutes or till golden. Remove from pans. Serve warm. Makes about 16 muffins.

leather belts stretched between floors, linking the milling machinery.

Gerald can count on experts at the town's big modern mill, Star of the West, for advice. "I can always call and say, 'Hey, what do I do now?'" Gerald grins.

Milling isn't an everyday affair here. The Frankenmuth Mill produces only enough flours, meals, and mixes to stock the shelves of its gift shop and those of a few other local stores. The mill's real job is to provide

visitors to this Bavarian-style town 60 miles north of Detroit with a peek at history. Signs throughout the mill describe the machinery and operation for those taking self-guided tours. The mill is open daily from 10 a.m. to 6 p.m. in summer.

For mill products and information, contact: *Frankenmuth Mill, 701 Mill St., Frankenmuth, MI 48734.*

Brownville Mills

The Brownville Mills' quiet exterior gives nary a hint of the old building's boisterous past.

Jesse James wouldn't recognize his old hangout, The Lone Tree Saloon. The 19th-century Brownville, Nebraska, watering hole that drew cardsharps, Missouri River rats, and ladies of questionable repute has grown virtuous in its old age. The building now houses the Brownville Mills, which—like the old-time saloon before it—takes great pride in being accommodating.

"If your hours don't fit our hours, let us know," says mill owner Harold Davis, who's been known to crawl out of bed in the middle of the night to satisfy a customer's yen for a bag of one of his specialty flours, such as triticale (a wheat/rye cross) or protein-rich amaranthe. Harold just as happily will grind you a fresh bag of cornmeal, or rice, rye, wheat, or buckwheat flour.

His devotion is rewarded: Many of Brownville Mills' customers are so faithful that Harold can predict when they'll drop by.

A search for a new market for the wheat he raised led this whole-grains enthusiast into milling, and eventually out of farming altogether.

continued

Brownville Corn Pancakes

For a tasty change of pace, stir up these corny flapjacks. They're almost as easy to make as pancakes from a mix.

- ⅔ cup stone-ground cornmeal
- ⅔ cup stone-ground corn flour
- 1 teaspoon cream of tartar
- ½ teaspoon baking soda
- ½ teaspoon salt
- 2 well-beaten eggs
- 1 cup milk
- ¼ cup safflower oil or cooking oil
  Margarine or butter
  Hot syrup

1. In a medium bowl, stir together cornmeal, corn flour, cream of tartar, baking soda, and salt.
2. In a small bowl, combine eggs, milk, and safflower or cooking oil. Add all at once to the flour mixture, stirring till batter is well mixed.
3. Keeping the batter in the bowl well stirred, pour about *2 tablespoons of the batter* for each pancake onto a hot, lightly greased griddle or heavy skillet. Cook till pancakes are golden brown, turning to cook other sides when pancakes have bubbly surfaces and slightly dry edges.
4. Serve corn pancakes with margarine *or* butter and hot syrup. Makes 16 to 20 pancakes.

Harold's Health Cookies

These Brownville Mills cookies are crunchy outside, chewy-soft inside, and delicious right down to the last bite.

  2 *eggs*
  1 *cup packed brown sugar*
  ½ *cup cane syrup, molasses, or*
      corn syrup
  ½ *cup honey*
2½ *cups stone-ground whole wheat flour*
  ½ *teaspoon baking soda*
  1 *teaspoon ground cinnamon*
  ½ *teaspoon ground cloves*
  ½ *teaspoon ground allspice*
  1 *cup shelled sunflower seeds*
  1 *cup sesame seed*
  1 *cup coarsely chopped pecans*
  1 *cup chopped raisins (optional)*

Miller Harold Davis relies on help from mom Darlene and son David.

In 1981, Harold bought the storefront mill, founded more than three decades ago by a magazine salesman who hoped to convert others to his passion for whole grains. "He was into natural foods back in the 50's," says Harold, who proudly claims the mill also is Nebraska's oldest health food store. Harold's two small electrically powered millstones grind only Midwest grains. "And I try to buy organically grown grains," he boasts.

In this tiny Missouri River town of 200 people (about 60 miles south of Omaha), the mill does a thriving mail-order trade. Harold depends on his mom Darlene and son David to help serve the steady clientele of walk-in customers. Many of them stop in Brownville (reputed to be the oldest town in Nebraska) to ride the riverboat or visit the museums and antiques and crafts shops.

Visitors also are welcome to watch Harold do the milling. The mill is open Mondays through Saturdays, from 9 a.m. to 5 p.m., and Sundays (May through November), from 2 p.m. to 5 p.m.

For mail orders, write or call: *Brownville Mills, Brownville NE 68321 (402/825-4131).*

1. In a large mixer bowl, combine eggs, brown sugar, syrup, and honey; beat well with an electric mixer. In a bowl, combine flour, baking soda, cinnamon, cloves, and allspice. Add to mixture; beat till well mixed.
2. By hand, stir in sunflower seeds, sesame seed, pecans, and raisins, if desired. (Dough may be covered and refrigerated for several hours or overnight.)
3. Drop dough from a teaspoon 2 inches apart onto a well-greased cookie sheet. Bake in a 325° oven for 10 to 12 minutes. Transfer cookies to a cooling rack. Makes about 96 cookies.

Bear's Mill

Terry and Julie Clark learned the art of milling grain the hard way, by restoring a 140-year-old Ohio mill piece by piece. Not that Bear's Mill, 35 miles northwest of Dayton, was in total disrepair. "Everything necessary was intact," Julie recalls. "That's not normal for an old mill—no dam washout or anything." Still, the mill, a four-story, weathered-walnut structure, hadn't been operating for five years. It was past time for a thorough cleanup and some tender, loving care.

Why would a young couple want to buy an old mill? "We didn't know a darn thing about milling," says Julie, who's a potter by trade. "And we knew very little about grain. Terry and I had an awful lot to learn." But the Clarks welcomed the challenge. "The kind of people who like pottery like mills," Julie winks.

More than a decade later, Julie and Terry are seasoned veterans. Callouses from toting heavy bags of grain mark their hands. The grain is hoisted to the mill's fourth floor, where it is cleaned. Then, it's held on the third floor in storage bins, till it's released to slide down to the second floor for grinding.

The Clarks know how to coax the best grinds of cornmeal and wheat

continued

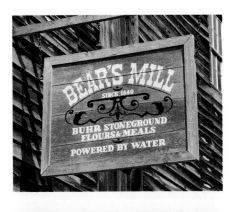

"Take it away," Mike shouts to Terry, working at their Ohio mill.

Rita's Applesauce Cake

This recipe comes from Rita Wiley, who works in the Bear's Mill pottery studio.

- 1 cup raisins
- 2½ cups all-purpose unbleached flour
- 2 cups sugar
- 1½ teaspoons baking soda
- ¾ teaspoon ground cinnamon
- ½ teaspoon baking powder
- ½ teaspoon ground cloves
- ½ cup margarine or butter, softened
- 1 large egg
- 1½ cups applesauce
- ½ cup chopped nuts

1. In a small saucepan, bring raisins and ¾ cup *water* to boiling; cover and simmer for 3 minutes. Remove from heat. Drain raisins, reserving liquid; if necessary, add additional water to liquid to make ½ cup. Chop raisins.
2. Meanwhile, in a large mixer bowl, stir together flour, sugar, soda, cinnamon, baking powder, cloves, and ½ teaspoon *salt*. Add margarine, egg, applesauce, and reserved raisin liquid.
3. Beat on low speed with an electric mixer till combined, then on medium speed for 2 minutes. Stir in nuts and raisins. Transfer to a greased and floured 13x9x2-inch baking pan.
4. Bake in a 350° oven for 45 to 50 minutes. Cool on a wire rack. Cut into squares. Top with *whipped cream,* if desired. Makes 12 to 15 servings.

Mike Johnson and Julie and Terry Clark.

Crunchy Cornmeal Cookies

A hint of lemon, a crunch of cornmeal—these blond cookies are one of Julie Clark's favorite recipes.

1½	cups sugar
1	cup shortening
2	eggs
¼	teaspoon lemon extract or 1 teaspoon lemon juice
2¾	cups soft, unbleached white flour or *cake flour*
1	cup cornmeal
1	teaspoon baking powder
1	teaspoon ground nutmeg
½	teaspoon salt
½	to 1 cup raisins

1. In a large mixer bowl, beat sugar, shortening, eggs, and lemon extract *or* lemon juice with an electric mixer till blended. In a bowl, stir together flour, cornmeal, baking powder, nutmeg, and salt. Add to shortening mixture and beat thoroughly. Stir in raisins.
2. Drop dough from a teaspoon 2 inches apart onto a greased cookie sheet. Bake in a 375° oven for 10 to 12 minutes. Transfer the cookies to a wire rack to cool. Makes 48 cookies.

flour from the massive millstones, imported from France and driven by water. They've even learned to fashion their own wooden replacement parts for the mill.

Julie and Terry live on the mill grounds in a made-over barn that houses the pottery studio. Julie sells her wares, as well as Bear's Mill flours and meals from the mill's shop.

A few years ago, they acquired a partner—Julie's brother Mike Johnson. For now, the mill operates only Thursdays through Sundays, but the partners hope someday to become full-time millers.

Terry grinds the grain on Saturdays, enveloping the mill in a pleasantly nutty, musty aroma—and camouflaging himself in a fine, ghost-white dust. Bear's Mill Hours: Thursdays, Fridays, and Sundays, from 11 a.m. to 5 p.m.; Saturdays, from 9 a.m. to 5 p.m.

For more information, write or call: *Bear's Mill, 6526 Arcanum-Bear's Mill Rd., Greenville, OH 45331 (513/548-5112).*

Rita's Applesauce Cake

Crunchy Cornmeal Cookies

FROM MIDWEST CANDY SHOPS
Sweet Secrets

It's Christmas—forget the diet! Who can resist these candy makers' chocolates, caramels, and creams? Learn their delicious secrets. Then, mix up a rich batch of your own holiday confections at home.

Now retired, Marie King leaves the candy making at her shop to son Jay.

When she scans the shelves brimming with crunchy brittle, caramel-nut clusters, and butter creams, Marie King's arms ache all over again. "I 'bout ruined my arms stirring so much," she sighs. Marie gave her arms a rest more than 13 years ago, when she turned over her spoon and candy shop, called Marie's Candies, to son Jay. Now he makes all the candy sold at Marie's, using Mom's secret recipes.

From Marie's farmhouse kitchen, where the candy making began in the 1950's, her shop moved to West Liberty, Ohio. Year-round, cars with out-of-town and out-of-state license plates buzz in and out of one of Logan County's busiest parking lots—next door to Marie's Candies. The butter creams alone—not to mention the peppermint chews and the caramels—explain the bumper-to-bumper crowds. Marie claims it's the rich butter, the cream with 40 percent butterfat (whipping cream is only 32 percent butterfat), and the roasted nuts that make her candies taste sublime.

WEST LIBERTY, OHIO
Marie's Candies

Marie's sells 30 tons of candy a year—one-third of it in December. From August on, Jay is at work by 5 a.m. and sometimes stays until midnight, getting set for the Christmas rush. His wife, three kids, and 25 holiday part-timers help out. "It's a little like having a baby," Jay laughs. "Right afterwards, you say, 'Never again.' But then, next year, you're ready!"

For more information on candy assortments, write to: *Marie's Candies, 311 Zanesfield Rd., West Liberty, OH 43357.*

Hard Candy

Color these confections festive red and green for the holidays.

2¼ cups sugar
½ cup light corn syrup
½ cup water
½ teaspoon oil of peppermint, orange, lemon, anise, cinnamon, wintergreen, cloves, or spearmint
Food coloring
Powdered sugar

1. Line an 8x8x2-inch baking pan with foil, extending foil over edges of pan. Oil or butter foil; set pan aside.
2. In a heavy 2-quart saucepan, combine sugar, corn syrup, and water. Cook and stir over high heat till mixture boils. Clip a candy thermometer to side of pan.
3. Continue cooking over medium heat, stirring occasionally, till thermometer registers 300° (hard-crack stage). Remove thermometer from pan; remove pan from heat. Add the desired flavoring and coloring. Immediately pour mixture into prepared pan. Let stand for 5 to 10 minutes or till a film forms over the candy surface.
4. Using a broad spatula, mark candy surface in ½-inch squares. *Do not break film on surface.* (If candy doesn't hold its shape, it isn't cool enough to mark. Let stand a few more minutes.)
5. Retrace previous lines, pressing spatula deeper each time, but not breaking the surface until the spatula can be pressed to the bottom along all lines. (If candy hardens before the pieces are cut, put it in a warm oven for a few minutes.)
6. Cool completely. Use foil to lift the candy out of the pan; break candy into squares. Roll candy pieces in powdered sugar; shake off excess. Makes 1 pound candy.

Caramels

Hard Candy

Caramels

Soft and buttery flavored, these caramels are rich and delicious. Yum!

1 16-ounce package brown sugar (2¼ cups packed)
2 cups light corn syrup
½ cup whipping cream
6 tablespoons butter
2 tablespoons whipping cream
½ teaspoon vanilla

1. Butter a 15x10x1-inch baking pan. Set prepared baking pan aside.
2. In a heavy 3-quart saucepan, combine brown sugar, corn syrup, and the ½ cup whipping cream; mix well. Cook over medium-high heat to boiling, stirring constantly to dissolve the sugar. Carefully clip candy thermometer to side of pan.
3. Cook over medium heat, stirring frequently, till candy thermometer registers 250° (hard-ball stage). Mixture should boil at a moderate, steady rate over the entire surface. Remove from heat. Remove the thermometer from pan.
4. Add the butter, the 2 tablespoons whipping cream, and the vanilla; mix well. Pour the mixture into the prepared baking pan. Cool.
5. Cut the candy into about 1½x½-inch rectangles. Roll each piece of candy in waxed paper or plastic wrap. Store candy, tightly covered, in a cool, dry place. Makes 2¼ pounds candy.

103

Heavenly Hash

Sauerkraut Candy

Caramels

Hard Candy

Chocolate Truffles

Almond Toffee

As usual, George Karandzieff is up to his wrists in chocolate—melting, stirring, and pouring it into his antique Santa molds. Since 1913, one Karandzieff or another has been making holiday Santas, angels, and divine Heavenly Hash at the family's Crown Candy Kitchen. It's St. Louis' most famous candy and ice cream emporium, complete with white wooden booths and a rainbow-colored jukebox.

Harry Karandzieff founded the business; now, grandsons Mike, Tom, and Andy run most of the show. But their dad George, a familiar face at Crown for 50 years, still has a hand in much of the candy making. "I just can't boogie out there like I used to," he laments with disgust, while seated near the chocolate melter in back of the family's combination candy shop, soda fountain, and lunch stop.

At Christmas, Crown Candy sells almost a half-ton of chocolates, from 3-inch elves to 2-foot-tall Santas made with antique molds. George considers the Santas, which weigh 7 pounds, works of art. He doesn't care if they sell or not—but they always do.

In seven-plus decades, Crown Candy has only closed down once—for a month after a fire in 1983. Offers to expand into glitzy new malls and to buy the shop are fairly commonplace. But the Karandzieffs remain at their modest digs in an off-the-beaten-path neighborhood. "Talk is cheap," says George about the offers. Mike just shakes his head: "People get hold of your business' name, then stick some manager in, and there goes your reputation." In this case, that's a lot to lose.

For information on Crown chocolates, nuts, and caramels, write to: *Crown Candy, 1401 St. Louis Ave., St. Louis, MO 63106.*

ST. LOUIS, MISSOURI

Crown Candy Kitchen

Sauerkraut Candy
Coconut makes this candy look shaggy.

  2 cups sugar
1½ cups light corn syrup
  2 tablespoons water
  6 cups shredded coconut
  2 tablespoons whipping cream
  1 tablespoon butter

1. Line a 13x9x2-inch baking pan with foil, extending foil over edges of pan. Butter the foil; set pan aside. In a Dutch oven or large heavy saucepan, combine sugar, corn syrup, and water. Cook and stir over medium-high heat till sugar is dissolved and mixture boils. Stir in coconut. Carefully clip candy thermometer to side of pan.

2. Cook and stir over medium-high heat till mixture reaches 238° (coconut should be lightly golden). Stir in cream. Continue cooking till mixture again reaches 238°. Stir in butter.

3. Pour into prepared pan. Cool slightly. Fluff with a fork. Cool. Cut candy into squares. Wrap in waxed paper. Do not stack candy. Makes about 2½ pounds candy.

Heavenly Hash

  1 pound milk chocolate
30 large marshmallows
  1 cup pecan halves

1. In the top of a double boiler set over simmering water or in a heavy saucepan over low heat, melt chocolate, stirring often till chocolate is smooth and reaches 90°.

2. Meanwhile, on a baking sheet, arrange *24* of the marshmallows in a single layer in blocks of six. Cut the 6 remaining marshmallows into eighths. Place pecans in a small saucepan.

3. When chocolate is ready, pour about ¼ cup (enough to cover) over each block of marshmallows. (White streaks in the chocolate mean it's too hot.) Stir about ½ cup of the melted chocolate into pecans; keep warm. Stir marshmallow pieces into remaining chocolate. Plug holes between large marshmallows with chocolate-covered marshmallow pieces. Spread pecan-chocolate mixture over top. Let candy stand till set.

4. To serve, break or cut candy into pieces. Makes 1¾ pounds candy.

Mostly Chocolate *RAPID CITY, SOUTH DAKOTA*

Decisions, decisions! Bavarian mint, raspberry, or Irish cream? Choosing which of 15 flavors of truffles to try can be downright troubling at the Mostly Chocolate candy shop in Rapid City.

The shop originally started by Wes Mostaert and now owned by Kelly Commet specializes in truffles. Kelly claims the best part of the business is hearing all the "oohs and aahs" when customers bite into one.

Surrounded by bowls of milk chocolate, dark chocolate, and ingredients such as mocha for the fillings, the shop's candy makers start their day of truffle making. In seven smooth steps, they mix the truffles, roll them by hand, and double-dip them in chocolate. Then, like the artists they are, they "sign" each one with its own design. As the candy making finishes, the shop fills with the irresistible aroma of chocolate. Kelly is so proud of the fragrance, she invites customers on her marquee, "Stop in just for the smell of it."

Besides the famous truffles, Mostly Chocolate sells other chocolate creations, too—pecan clusters, chocolate-dipped apricots, and almond toffee.

For information on gift-boxed assortments of candies, write to: *Mostly Chocolate, 2926 W. Flormann, Rapid City, SD 57702.*

Almond Toffee

It's nutty, crunchy, and smothered with chocolate.

  1 cup butter*
  1 cup sugar
  1 tablespoon water
  ¾ cup finely chopped toasted almonds
  4 to 5 ounces milk chocolate, coarsely chopped

1. Line a 13x9x2-inch baking pan with foil, extending foil over edges. Butter the pan.
2. In a heavy 2-quart saucepan, melt the butter. Add sugar and water. Cook and stir over medium-high heat to boiling. Clip candy thermometer to side of pan. Continue cooking, stirring frequently, over medium heat till thermometer registers 295° (hard-crack stage). Watch carefully after 280° to prevent scorching. Remove from heat. Remove the thermometer. Stir in ½ cup of the toasted almonds.
3. Quickly pour candy into prepared pan; spread quickly and evenly. Let stand about 2 minutes or till partially set. Slide foil and candy out of pan and onto countertop. Cover candy, using Topping Method I or II. Makes 1¼ pounds candy.
Topping Method I: Sprinkle chopped chocolate over the top of the hot candy. When it's melted, spread chocolate over the candy. Sprinkle with remaining almonds. Cool candy; break into pieces.
Topping Method II: Score candy into 2x2-inch pieces. Cut and separate pieces; cool till firm. Melt chocolate; spread on tops of pieces. Sprinkle with remaining almonds. (At Mostly Chocolate, toffee squares are dipped into melted chocolate.)
Note: Be sure to use real butter in toffee. With margarine, the fat separates out onto the candy's surface.

Almond Toffee

Chocolate Truffles

Chocolate Truffles

Even neophytes can master this simplified recipe.

 12 ounces milk chocolate, finely chopped (don't use milk chocolate pieces)
  ¼ cup whipping cream
  ¼ cup sifted unsweetened cocoa powder or ⅓ cup finely chopped toasted almonds, pecans, or walnuts

1. Place chocolate in a small saucepan. In another small saucepan, heat whipping cream just to boiling, stirring constantly. Pour over chocolate; cover pan and let stand for 3 to 4 minutes or till chocolate melts. Stir till blended, smooth, and glossy. (The mixture may look curdled, but keep stirring and it becomes smooth.) Cover and refrigerate about 15 minutes or till well chilled.
2. Drop by rounded teaspoonfuls onto a waxed-paper-lined baking sheet. Cover loosely; refrigerate for 1 hour.
3. With palms of hands, roll each piece of candy into a ball. Roll balls in the cocoa powder or chopped nuts to coat evenly. Serve candy at room temperature. To store, place in an airtight container in the refrigerator for up to 1 week. Makes about 1 pound candy (20 pieces).
Mint-Chocolate Truffles: Follow the recipe above, *except* stir in ¼ teaspoon *mint extract* after the chocolate and whipping cream have been blended.
Orange-Chocolate Truffles: Follow the recipe above, *except* stir in 1 teaspoon *orange extract* after the chocolate and whipping cream have been blended. Substitute 1 cup toasted *coconut* for the cocoa powder.

 *Discover the bounty that's for sale in the Heartland. Come with us to some of the most colorful Midwest markets. Pick through the spectacular fruits, vegetables, baked goods, cheeses, fish, poultry, and meats that city markets in Cleveland, St. Louis, Indianapolis, and Detroit have to offer. Or, if country goodness is more your style, shop with us at the Dane County Market in Wisconsin, the Princeton Market in Illinois, or the Mennonite Relief Auction in Kansas. As we visit, we'll introduce you to some of the folks who work at the markets—people such as produce experts Lawrence Zienert and Wilbur Smith in Detroit, chicken man John Roston in Cleveland, and volunteer Marie Litwiller of Hopedale, Illinois, who bakes for the Mennonite Sale in Peoria. They'll be glad to share their knowledge as well as their favorite recipes. Once you've met all of these fine folks and experienced the markets for yourself, we think you'll find the sights, sounds, aromas, people, and foods so fascinating,*

Markets

you'll want to return and savor them again and again.

Fresh-from-the-Farm Goodness

Farmers markets glory in the homegrown bounty of the rural Midwest.

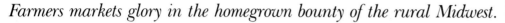

Bargains by the bushel. Freshness straight from the farm. A rainbow of glossy green watermelons, sun-yellow sweet corn, and rosy red tomatoes, plucked from their stalks and vines just hours before. That's but a hint of the bounty at markets all across the Midwest.

Join us as we browse and bargain at Detroit's big 100-year-old Eastern Market, the Dane County Farmers' Market around Madison's Capitol Square in Wisconsin, and the neighborly, small-town market in Princeton, Illinois.

Going to market: Eastern Market, Russell just off Gratiot Avenue, open Mondays–Saturdays year-round; Dane County Market, Madison's Capitol Square, open Wednesdays and Saturdays from late April through October; Princeton Market, city-hall park, open Tuesdays and Saturdays mid-July through October.

Bountiful Buys

"During the winter, I watch the produce clerk sprinkling those sad-looking supermarket vegetables. I cry for this," exclaims an exuberant shopper, her arms heavy with carrots and squash. Dirt still clinging to the roots and a hint of dew on the stems prove the produce indeed arrived farm fresh that very morning. "You know how much these would cost in the grocery store?" the shopper whispers, handing $4 to the farmer for a bargain bushel of peppers. "Two dollars a quart!"

Faithful Farmers

At Detroit, Madison, Princeton, and locations all around the Midwest, farmers market connections go way back—sometimes three, even four, generations. "There's no place like the market," proclaims Lawrence Zienert, who's sold produce from the same stall at Detroit's market for 60 years. Wilbur Smith agrees. He makes the 50-mile trip daily from his Erie, Michigan, farm to Detroit, as he's done for more than 50 years. His grandsons join him now. "A fella and I were talking about the market. I told him it gets in your blood," Wilbur pauses. "He said maybe I need a transfusion."

(Opposite) Since 1890, arriving early and bargaining for the best prices have been rules of the game at Detroit's Eastern Market. (Above) Buying vegetables is fun. You can chat with folks who grow them. Most farmers in Detroit give samples. (Right) Detroit's market means fun for Nicholas Dearsman.

111

Farmers Market Tips

Take along more than a canvas bag when you go thumping, sniffing, and poking your way through farmers markets. Armed with our tips, you'll bring home only the freshest, tastiest fruits and vegetables.

SUREFIRE FRESHNESS TESTS
Instead of stuffing the first foot-long zucchini you see into your shopping bag, know the tests for ripeness, tenderness, and maturity.

Broccoli Look for firm stalks with deep green or purplish green heads that are tightly packed. Heads that are light green or that have tiny yellow flowers are past their prime.

Cantaloupe Look for a firm, tan melon with heavy netting on the rind and a sweet smell. Avoid melons with rough stem ends. On vine-ripened melons (the best kind), stems fall off during harvest.

Cauliflower Heads should be heavy and solid with bright green leaves. Avoid cauliflower with brown bruises, a speckled appearance, or yellow, withered leaves.

Corn Look for brown, dried silks and ears wrapped firmly in green husks. Then use the thumbnail test. If a milky fluid squirts out when you puncture a kernel, the corn is just right. (The fluid is clear, not milky, in high-sugar varieties.)

Cucumber For salads, choose firm cucumbers without shriveled or soft spots. Choose smaller cucumbers for pickling.

Lettuce and cabbage Choose solid, heavy heads, but not necessarily the biggest ones. Dark green lettuce is higher in vitamins than light-colored lettuce.

Peach Choose peaches that are firm to slightly soft when pressed. Skin color varies from golden yellow to dark reddish brown, but the peaches should have no tinges of green. Look for well-shaped fruit without blemishes or soft spots.

Squash Summer squash (zucchini, crookneck, and straightneck varieties) should be no more than 8 inches long, with a firm, glossy skin. Squash that's too ripe has big seeds, stringy flesh, and may even be hollow.

Tomatoes Buy tomatoes that aren't completely ripe, along with ripe ones. That way, you'll have a steady supply until your next farmers market excursion. Let tomatoes ripen on the kitchen counter out of direct sunlight. Then refrigerate them as soon as they're ripe.

Watermelon When you thump a melon, listen for a dull thud, rather than a ring, which indicates an immature melon. (One Iowa grower thumps his melons, then his head, and pronounces his melons ready for harvest when the thumps sound the same!) Other signs of ripeness: a dull-looking rind with a yellowish underside and a dark, crisp stem.

HANDLE WITH CARE!
Get your produce home as quickly as you can. Perishable vegetables don't tolerate hot cars, so make the farmers market the last stop on your errand list. Shop early in the day for the best choices, and head for vendors whose produce is shaded. If the day is a scorcher, take along an ice chest.
❖ Don't wash vegetables until you're ready to serve them (unwashed produce keeps better).
❖ Most, but not all, produce should be refrigerated in your crisper compartment or in plastic bags punched with a few air holes (husk corn before refrigerating it).
❖ Put potatoes in a cool, dark place. Refrigeration turns them from starchy to sweet.

If pesticides are a concern, here's your chance to find out about growers' practices. Don't be bashful about wanting to know varieties, either. Certain types of tomatoes and cucumbers, say, are better for canning than others.

Be snoopy about when the produce was picked. Obviously, fresher is better, especially when it comes to peas and most varieties of sweet corn, which lose sweetness rapidly after harvest. Timing also is critical with picking cucumbers. When buying cucumbers, follow grandma's old rule: "24 hours from vine to brine."

Many growers can tell you how to prepare what you buy—especially varieties that are new to you. Who knows, you may get some great tips and recipes from the folks who grew that spaghetti squash!

(Top) Mennonite Jim Fitz proudly sells produce at the Princeton, Illinois, market. (Bottom) Princeton's market is small-town friendly. John Welsh sells produce here on Saturdays and at his roadside stand during the week.

113

FRESH FLAVORS AND AROMAS FROM
City Markets

Pungent with earthy odors of fresh produce, briny aromas of fish, and sweet smells of baking breads, city markets sweep you up in their clamorous bustle. Since trading-post days, they've served as crossroads for the Midwest's many cultures.

Exploring these markets is an adventure. Grab your biggest basket and join us in Cleveland, St. Louis, and Indianapolis. You'll meet people who get up before dawn to peddle their wares, and you'll take home tempting recipes from folks who make selling good things to eat their business.

Some visitors go to Cleveland's West Side Market just for the people show. The stars include plump, Slavic grandmothers—babushkas tied snugly around their gray-haired heads—expertly elbowing young, well-tailored "yuppie gourmets" away from the meatiest peppers.

You can see cheese vendors proffering samples of irresistible Amish cheeses and bakers creating

West Side Market

CLEVELAND, OHIO

Vendors at Cleveland's bustling West Side Market are proud of the products they sell. They have good reason. The items found at the market are some of the best of the Midwest.

crowds around their golden loaves just by fanning the yeasty aromas into the aisles.

Clevelanders love Saturday mornings at their 80-year-old, city-owned market in Ohio City, Cleveland's old ethnic neighborhood on the west bank of the Cuyahoga River. Roaming from butcher to baker to egg man under the massive arched ceiling, customers find more than 70 vendors representing more than 20 ethnic cuisines. Old-world delicacies abound, from homemade rice sausage and colorful headcheese to sauerkraut-filled pirogies and babka, a sweet Polish bread.

CLAMOR UNDER THE CUPOLA

Imported pastas, fresh-from-the-farm melons, and iced-down fish fill the mammoth market (designed, it's said, to architecturally mimic the

ancient Roman Colosseum). Depression-era Works Progress Administration murals spill forth luscious ripe fruits, and ceramic friezes depict oceans of shellfish and gardens of vegetables. Livestock decorate the capitals on each one of the building's interior columns.

John F. Rolston, a chef who works at his family's poultry stand, says he enjoys helping his customers select the turkeys, chickens, and geese served at special family events. His creation, Poulet au Vin Blanc (see recipe, page 118), superbly demonstrates his culinary expertise with poultry.

At Michael's Bakery, European-style breads and pastries lure customers. Michael Mitterholzer's success comes from knowing his Russian, German, and Slovak patrons. "We have the type of bread they're used to," he says.

Born in Czechoslovakia, Mike emigrated to Cleveland at age 17. "After the war, things were so bad that I wanted to be either a butcher or a baker so I could have something to eat," he says.

Mike's Bienenstich, glazed with almonds and honey and filled with a sweet, creamy custard, makes a big hit with the baker's hundreds of loyal customers (see recipe, page 118).

The West Side Market, at West 25th and Lorain Avenue, is open Mondays and Wednesdays, from 7 a.m. to 4 p.m.; Fridays and Saturdays, from 7 a.m. to 6 p.m. Holiday hours may vary.

The colorful West Side Market has something for everyone. Shoppers can take their pick of garden-fresh produce, zesty cheeses, plump chickens, delicious breads and pastries, or anything in between.

117

Mike Mitterholzer's Bienenstich

1 14-ounce loaf frozen sweet bread
     dough, thawed
½ cup sliced almonds, toasted
¼ cup sugar
3 tablespoons butter
1 tablespoon water
1 tablespoon honey
⅓ cup sugar
2 tablespoons cornstarch
1¼ cups milk
1 tablespoon butter
1 tablespoon shortening
3 slightly beaten egg yolks
1 teaspoon vanilla

1. On a lightly floured surface, roll out dough to form a 12x7-inch rectangle. Place in a greased 12x7½x2-inch baking dish.
2. In a saucepan, combine almonds, ¼ cup sugar, 3 tablespoons butter, water, and honey. Cook and stir till bubbly. Spread over dough. Cover; let rise in a warm place for 30 minutes or till nearly doubled. Place dish in a shallow baking pan.
3. Bake in a 350° oven for 25 to 30 minutes. Cool in dish for 10 minutes. Remove from dish; cool.
4. Meanwhile, for custard, in another saucepan, combine the ⅓ cup sugar and cornstarch. Stir in the milk, then add 1 tablespoon butter and shortening. Cook and stir till bubbly. Cook and stir for 2 minutes more.
5. Gradually stir about *half* of the hot mixture into the yolks. Return all to saucepan. Cook and stir till nearly bubbly. Reduce heat. Cook for 2 minutes more. (Do not boil.) Remove saucepan from heat. Stir in vanilla. Cover surface with waxed paper. Let cool slightly (30 minutes).
6. Split bread in half. Fill with custard. Cover; refrigerate for 3 to 24 hours. Cut into squares. Serves 9.

Poulet au Vin Blanc

Chef John Rolston creates this French dish from chickens his father sells at Cleveland's West Side Market.

Herbed Rice
1 tablespoon cooking oil
½ teaspoon dried thyme, crushed
4 skinned and boned chicken-breast
     halves
1½ cups sliced fresh mushrooms
¼ cup dry white wine
¼ cup whipping cream
1 tablespoon butter

1. Prepare rice. Cover; keep warm.
2. In a large skillet, combine cooking oil and thyme. Cook the chicken in the hot oil mixture for 2 to 3 minutes or till brown. Turn; cook chicken for 3 minutes more.
3. Sprinkle mushrooms around chicken. Add wine. Cook, uncovered, over medium-high heat for 3 minutes.
4. Add whipping cream and butter. Cook, uncovered, over medium-high heat for 2 to 3 minutes more or till sauce thickens slightly.
5. Serve chicken and sauce over rice. Makes 4 servings.
Herbed Rice: In a saucepan, mix 1½ cups *chicken broth*, ⅓ cup *long-grain rice*, 2 tablespoons sliced *scallions*, and ⅛ teaspoon *dried thyme, crushed*. Bring to boiling; reduce heat. Cover; simmer for 20 minutes. Remove from heat. Let stand, covered, for 10 minutes.

Soulard Market

The morning's first light reveals Joe Monte hastily stacking cucumbers and piling tomatoes in crimson pyramids. Though the new day barely has broken, Joe knows he's only minutes ahead of his first customers. By 6:30 a.m., St. Louis' Soulard Market, the over 200-year-old landmark only 2 miles south of downtown, starts swarming with shoppers.

Soulard, St. Louis' oldest neighborhood, is a community of two-family flats, lodge halls, factories, and spired churches. Its heart, however, remains the market area, a complex of indoor and outdoor stalls where vendors coax customers to their dewy mounds of produce.

Joe sold his first pound of tomatoes at the ripe old age of 6. That was in 1926. "In those days," he reminisces, "there were more live animals—pigs, cows, goats, rabbits, and crawdads. Everything had to be fresh. You couldn't give away a butchered chicken."

Like Joe, most Soulard merchants have deep roots at the market. Their fathers and grandfathers—many of them European immigrants—taught them the business.

EARLY BIRDS GET THE BEST

Some merchants grow all their produce and truck it into town themselves. Others buy at the city's

continued

wholesale market, Produce Row. "You have to get up early and really shop around to get a jump on your competitors," says Joe, who makes his choices with a cook's keen eye.

It's a competitive environment, but it's also convivial. "We make a living," says cheese man Ben Abkemeira, "but mostly people like me just like being here." So, too, do the throngs who gather at the produce stalls, meat markets, snack bars, bakery, and spice shop. Joe is certain the Soulard Market will survive as long as customers believe the vendors' eternal credo: "The meat and produce that you find in the grocery stores always will look better than they really taste."

Soulard Market, 730 Carroll Street, is open Mondays–Fridays, from 8:00 a.m. to 5:00 p.m., and Saturdays, from 6:00 a.m. to 5:30 p.m.

Vanilla Nut Cake

Linda Nolle, veteran spice vendor at St. Louis' Soulard Market, says, "I like this cake because it's not too sweet. It's delicious with sorbet or ice cream."

- 3 cups all-purpose flour
- ½ teaspoon salt
- ½ cup margarine
- ½ cup butter
- ¼ cup cooking oil
- 3 cups sugar
- 5 large eggs
- 1 5-ounce can evaporated milk (⅔ cup)
- ⅓ cup water
- 1 tablespoon vanilla
- 1 tablespoon butter flavoring
- ⅛ teaspoon yellow food coloring (optional)
- ½ cup pecan meal or ground pecans
- ½ cup chopped pecans
  Icing (optional)
  Pecan halves (optional)

1. In a bowl, combine flour and salt. In a mixer bowl, beat margarine, butter, and cooking oil with an electric mixer for 30 seconds. Add sugar; beat till fluffy.
2. Add the eggs, one at a time; beat 1 minute after each. In a bowl, combine evaporated milk, water, vanilla, butter flavoring, and food coloring, if desired. Alternately, add liquid and flour mixtures to beaten mixture; beating till the mixture is combined.
3. In a well-greased, 10-inch tube pan, sprinkle the meal or ground nuts, coating bottom and sides of pan. Spread chopped nuts over bottom. Turn batter into pan.
4. Bake in a 325° oven for 1¾ hours. Cool for 15 minutes. Remove cake

from pan. Cool on a wire rack.
5. Drizzle cake with Icing, if desired. Decorate top with pecan halves, if desired. Makes 12 servings.
Icing: In a bowl, combine ½ cup sifted *powdered sugar*, ½ teaspoon *vanilla*, and 2 to 3 teaspoons *milk* to make an icing of drizzling consistency.

Joe Monte's Marinated Roast Peppers

- 6 to 8 medium sweet red and/or green peppers, halved and seeded
  Olive oil
- ¼ cup olive oil
- 2 tablespoons vinegar
- ½ teaspoon Italian seasoning
- ¼ teaspoon salt
- ⅛ teaspoon pepper

1. Brush pepper halves with some olive oil. Place halves, cut side down, on an unheated rack of a broiler pan*. Flatten slightly, splitting as necessary. Broil 3 inches from the heat until surfaces char. Place in a brown paper bag; let cool. Remove and discard skin. Cut into ½-inch-wide strips.
2. In a medium mixing bowl, combine the ¼ cup olive oil, vinegar, Italian seasoning, salt, and pepper. Add broiled pepper strips. Cover; chill for 2 to 24 hours. Makes 10 to 12 servings.
*Note: Instead of broiling, you can roast the peppers by placing them in a 15x10x1-inch baking pan and baking them in a 450° oven for about 20 minutes or till charred.

SOULARD
FARMER'S
MARKET
SINCE 1779

NORTON SUPREME
California STRAWBERRIES

NORTON SUPREME
California STRAWBERRIES

John Walker's Hash-Brown Quiche

3 cups loose-pack, frozen hash-brown
    potatoes, thawed
⅓ cup butter, melted
6 ounces diced cooked ham
    (about 1 cup)
4 ounces hot pepper cheese, shredded
4 ounces gouda or Swiss cheese,
    shredded (1 cup)
½ cup light cream
2 eggs
¼ teaspoon seasoned salt

1. Press hash browns between paper towels to remove moisture. Press hash browns onto bottom and up sides of a 9-inch pie plate to form a crust.
2. Drizzle melted butter over crust. Bake in a 425° oven for 25 minutes. Remove from oven. Reduce oven temperature to 350°.
3. In a bowl, toss together the ham and cheeses. Place ham mixture in crust. Beat together cream, eggs, and seasoned salt. Pour cream mixture over ham mixture.
4. Bake, uncovered, in the 350° oven for 25 to 30 minutes or till a knife inserted near the center comes out clean. Let stand for 10 minutes before serving. Makes 6 servings.

John Walker's Hash-Brown Quiche

A jazz trio serenades from the balcony of the Indianapolis City Market with a bouncy rendition of the tune "Easy Living." Below, Mike Raimondi upends a watering can over his brussels sprouts.

"Need anything today?" asks his wife Ann for the hundredth time, as she dries her hands on a towel. "Anything at all?"

And you can find practically anything—from celery hearts to egg rolls—at the Indianapolis City Market, a trading center that began in the 1800s as a hay market.

Bathed in sunlight from an arcade of windows under the roof's soaring ridge line and the elaborately mullioned Gothic windows at both ends, the market house seems almost like a cathedral.

The atmosphere inside, though, resembles a county fair, with restaurants, fishmongers, and shoe-shine shops side by side.

MEET THE CHEESE WIZARD

How long has Walker Cheese been part of this scene? "Oh, only 47 years," chuckles John Walker.

John's fame rests on his cheese "torte" of blue, cheddar, and port wine/cheddar rolled in chopped nuts. He uses his own favorite combo—Gouda, Swiss, and hot pepper—however, for his Hash-Brown Quiche (see recipe, opposite).

Tucked into a corner of the main market house is the aromatic Athens Imported Foods shop. Here customers find a little bit of everything—all of it Mediterranean. Bulging burlap sacks of lima beans, lentils, and steel-cut (not rolled and flaked) oats share shelf space with a half-dozen varieties of Spanish and Greek olives, fresh feta, and olive oil. The shop also sells delicious, ready-made baklava, stuffed grape leaves, spanokopitta, and other delicacies.

For more than two decades store employees have been doing what they enjoy most—sharing tidbits of Mediterranean culture with visitors and explaining what goes into a real Greek meal. Shoppers usually leave munching on a dried apricot or Greek olive.

Indianapolis City Market, located at Market and Alabama streets in the downtown area (just across the street from the Market Square Arena), stays open from 6 a.m. to 3:30 p.m. Mondays–Saturdays. It's closed Sundays.

Cheese whiz John Walker with Athens Imported Foods founder George Nikou.

INDIANAPOLIS, INDIANA

City Market

(Top) At Athens Imported Foods, you can find just about anything you need to make a Greek recipe. (Bottom) Mike Raimoni weighs some produce for a customer at his market stall.

Pasticcio with Kima

This traditional Greek dish is a particular favorite of George Nikou and his wife. George founded Athens Imported Foods in the Indianapolis City Market over 20 years ago.

- 1 *pound ground lamb* and/or *beef*
- 1 *cup chopped onion*
- ¼ *cup dry white wine*
- 2 *tablespoons tomato puree*
- ½ *cup fine dry bread crumbs*
- 12 *ounces elbow macaroni*
- ¼ *cup butter*
- 3 *slightly beaten egg whites*
- 1 *cup shredded mild white cheese*
  Dry bread crumbs
- ½ *cup butter*
- 1 *cup all-purpose flour*
- 1 *teaspoon salt*
- ¼ *teaspoon ground nutmeg (the Nikous use grated fresh nutmeg)*
- 3 *cups milk*
- ½ *cup shredded mild white cheese*
- 3 *slightly beaten egg yolks*
- ½ *cup shredded mild white cheese*

1. For Kima sauce, in a large skillet, cook lamb and/or beef and onion till meat is brown and onion is tender. Drain off fat. Stir in dry white wine and tomato puree. Cover and simmer the mixture for 10 minutes. Stir in ½ cup fine dry bread crumbs.
2. Meanwhile, cook the elbow macaroni according to package directions. Drain and return the macaroni to the saucepan. Stir in the ¼ cup butter. Stir in the egg whites and 1 cup shredded mild white cheese.
3. Butter a 13x9x2-inch baking dish. Sprinkle with some additional fine dry bread crumbs. Transfer the macaroni mixture to the baking dish. Spoon the Kima sauce mixture over the macaroni in baking dish.
4. In another saucepan, melt ½ cup butter. Stir in flour, salt, and nutmeg. Add milk all at once. Cook and stir till thickened and bubbly. Remove from heat. Stir in ½ cup cheese till melted. Add about *1 cup* of the hot mixture to the egg yolks. Return all to the saucepan. Pour over meat in the casserole, spreading to the edge.
5. Bake the casserole in a 350° oven for 25 minutes. Sprinkle the mixture with the remaining ½ cup shredded mild white cheese. Bake for 15 to 20 minutes more or till golden. Cool the casserole slightly and cut it into squares to serve. Makes 8 servings.

FROM MIDWEST MENNONITE COMMUNITIES
Old-Country Foods And Flavors

There's an abundance of great eating—strictly home cooking—at the 12 annual Mennonite Relief Auctions in the Midwest. Break away from the bill of fare and you also can buy handcrafted items, from grandfather clocks to stuffed toys. The dollars go to feed the hungry, with millions raised since the auctions first began in the 1950s. So dig deep in your pockets and get set to enjoy the food, the fun, and that extra-warm feeling that comes from helping others at the sales in Hutchinson, Kansas, and Peoria, Illinois.

Hutchinson, Kansas

The Kauffmans' Apple Butter

Edward and Frieda Kauffman of Haven, Kansas, make a huge batch of this spread every year for the Hutchinson auction. It's the best apple butter we've ever tasted!

> 6 pounds Jonathan apples (or other cooking apples)
> 4 cups water
> 8 cups apple cider
> 3 cups sugar

Apple butter bubbles up sweetly from a massive copper kettle Edward Kauffman has been tending since 4:30 a.m. The 80-year-old farmer from Haven, Kansas, a white apron covering his bib overalls, started before dawn in a makeshift kitchen at the Kansas State Fairgrounds in Hutchinson.

There'll be 1,000 jars of his creation at the Mennonite Relief Sale. Handsewn quilts, crafts from Kansas and around the world, and heirlooms to be auctioned also entice more than 30,000 bidders to the two-day event. It's sponsored by at least 65 southwest Kansas Amish, Mennonite, and Brethren in Christ congregations. (The denominations share similar roots, though they've grown in different directions.)

Money raised, in Hutchinson, more than $4.5 million over the years, goes to feed the needy.

Volunteers do all the work, and everything is donated—from dairy cows sold at the livestock auction to thick slabs of homemade pie. Just cooking and serving all the food requires at least 1,000 helpers.

Only the state fair brings more visitors to Hutchinson, and young and old alike eagerly await the sale.

(Above and opposite) *Edward Kauffman uses 50 bushels of apples in his apple butter.*

This day, patrons cheerfully pull jackets tighter against the chill and dodge puddles as early April sunshine melts yesterday's surprise snow. Broad-brimmed black hats and somber dress, common in Amish communities, mingle with Sunday-best spring pastels and cowboy hats.

People return to Hutchinson year after year because they want to help. But they

continued

1. Core and quarter unpeeled apples. In an 8- to 10-quart heavy Dutch oven, combine apples and water. Bring to boiling; reduce heat. Cover and simmer for 30 minutes, stirring occasionally.

2. Drain off liquid. Press apples through a cone-shaped colander or food mill. Discard the peels.

3. Meanwhile, in a large saucepan, cook the apple cider over high heat about 30 minutes or till cider is reduced by half.

4. In the Dutch oven, combine cooked apple mixture and reduced cider. Bring to boiling; reduce heat. Simmer, uncovered, for 30 minutes, stirring occasionally.

5. Stir in sugar. Bring to boiling; reduce heat. Simmer, uncovered, for 2 to 3 hours or till mixture resembles thick applesauce, stirring often. (It will thicken as it stands.)

6. Carefully ladle the hot mixture into sterilized, hot, half-pint jars, leaving ¼-inch headspace. Adjust lids. Process in boiling-water canner for 5 minutes. (Begin timing when water starts to boil.) Makes 6 to 8 half-pints.

Note: If you like, spoon the cooled apple butter into freezer containers. Seal, label, and freeze. You also can store it in the refrigerator.

also can't resist the heaping helpings of dishes their Russian, German, and Swiss ancestors brought to the Plains generations ago. Sale-goers may never sample some of these treats anywhere else.

Visitors pile plates high with goodies that include New Year's Cookies, a doughnutlike confection (volunteers make 40,000), and Verenika, a cheese-filled dumpling (see recipes, pages 130 and 136).

Verenika probably originated in old Russia, guesses Pat Stucky of Moundridge, Kansas, carrying an armload of the dumplings. "I married into this," she says and laughs. "We look forward to eating Verenika all year."

continued on page 132

Hutchinson Beef Borscht

Volunteers stir up this hearty sale dish.

1 pound lean beef chuck, trimmed of
    fat and cut into ¾-inch pieces
2 tablespoons cooking oil
3 cups water
1 or 2 bay leaves
3 cups coarsely chopped cabbage
2 cups peeled and cubed potatoes
½ cup chopped onion
¼ cup chopped green pepper
1 tablespoon dried parsley flakes
1 tablespoon instant beef bouillon
    granules
½ teaspoon dried dillweed
1 16-ounce can tomatoes, cut up
¼ cup light cream

1. In a large kettle or Dutch oven, brown the meat, half at a time, in hot cooking oil. Return all meat to the kettle. Add water and bay leaves. Bring to boiling; reduce heat. Cover and simmer for 50 to 60 minutes or till the meat is nearly tender.
2. Stir in cabbage, potatoes, onion, green pepper, parsley flakes, beef bouillon granules, and dillweed. Bring to boiling; reduce heat. Cover and simmer for 25 to 30 minutes more or till meat and potatoes are tender. Stir in the tomatoes; heat through. Remove from heat.
3. Season to taste with *salt* and *pepper*. Stir in light cream and remove bay leaves. Makes 6 servings.

New Year's Cookies

These doughnutlike pastries, fresh from the fryer, sell like hotcakes at the Mennonite sale in Hutchinson, Kansas.

⅓ cup warm water (105° to 115°)
2 packages active dry yeast
2 tablespoons sugar
¼ cup milk
2 tablespoons butter or *margarine*
2 slightly beaten eggs
1¾ cups all-purpose flour
½ teaspoon salt
¾ cup raisins
2 tablespoons all-purpose flour
Cookie Glaze or sugar (optional)
Shortening or *cooking oil for deep-fat frying*

1. In a small bowl, combine the warm water, yeast, and sugar. Let mixture stand about 5 minutes or till bubbly.
2. In a saucepan, heat milk and butter or margarine till butter is almost melted.
3. In a large mixing bowl, beat yeast mixture, milk mixture, eggs, 1¾ cups flour, and salt for 3 minutes.
4. Rinse raisins with *water*. Drain. Toss raisins with the 2 tablespoons flour. Beat into the dough. (Dough will be sticky.)
5. Make the Cookie Glaze, if desired.
6. To fry, drop dough by heaping teaspoons, 5 or 6 at a time, into deep, hot fat (365°). Fry for 2 minutes, turning once.
7. Drain on paper towels. Coat with glaze or sugar while warm. Makes 48.
Cookie Glaze: Beat together 4 cups sifted *powdered sugar*, 2 teaspoons *vanilla*, and enough *milk* (6 to 8 tablespoons) to make a thin glaze.

Peoria Rhubarb Cream Pie

This rich pie is a big hit at the Peoria, Illinois, relief sale.

Pastry for Single-Crust Pie
1½ cups sugar
¼ cup all-purpose flour
¾ teaspoon ground nutmeg
3 slightly beaten eggs
4 cups sliced fresh rhubarb or *thawed and drained frozen sliced rhubarb*
½ cup all-purpose flour
¼ cup sugar
⅓ cup butter or *margarine*

1. Prepare the pastry.
2. In a large bowl, combine 1½ cups sugar, ¼ cup flour, and nutmeg.
3. Add the eggs and mix well. Gently stir in the rhubarb. Turn the mixture into a pastry-lined pie plate.
5. In a small bowl, combine ½ cup flour and ¼ cup sugar. Cut in butter or margarine till mixture resembles coarse crumbs. Sprinkle over the pie.
6. Cover edge of pie with foil to prevent overbrowning. Bake in a 400° oven for 20 minutes. Remove foil. Bake about 20 minutes more or till topping is golden. Makes 1 pie.
Pastry for Single-Crust Pie: In a bowl, stir together 1¼ cups all-purpose *flour* and ¼ teaspoon *salt*. Cut in ⅓ cup *shortening* till pieces are the size of small peas. Using 3 to 4 tablespoons cold *water*, sprinkle *1 tablespoon* of the water over part of mixture; gently toss with a fork. Push to side of bowl. Repeat till all is moistened. Form dough into a ball.

On a lightly floured surface, flatten dough with hands. Roll dough from center to edges, forming a 12-inch circle. Ease pastry into a 9-inch pie plate, being careful not to stretch pastry. Trim to ½ inch beyond edge of pie plate; fold under extra pastry. Flute edge; *do not prick pastry.*

Aunt Anna Ulrich's Rolls

Hilda Heiser of Dewey, Illinois, makes these rolls for the Peoria sale.

1 package active dry yeast
⅔ cup warm water (105° to 115°)
⅔ cup mashed potato (about 1 large)
⅔ cup cooled potato water (from cooking potato)
1 tablespoon sugar
¾ teaspoon salt
2 eggs
⅔ cup sugar
⅔ cup lard or *shortening*
4½ to 5 cups all-purpose flour

1. In a large bowl, soften the yeast in the warm water.
2. Stir in the mashed potato, potato water, 1 tablespoon sugar, and salt. Cover and let stand at room temperature for 1 hour.
3. In a bowl, combine eggs, ⅔ cup sugar, and lard or shortening. Add to yeast mixture. Beat in enough flour to make a moderately soft dough. Cover and refrigerate overnight.
4. Punch dough down. Turn out onto a generously floured surface. Cover dough and let rest for 10 minutes.
5. Divide into 24 balls. With floured hands, shape as desired into rolls. (Dough will be sticky.) Place on greased baking sheets. Cover and let rise in a warm place till nearly double (30 to 45 minutes). Bake in a 375° oven about 12 minutes or till golden brown. Makes 24 rolls.

Wonderful recipes and great eating are a part of all the Mennonite Relief Auctions. Peoria Rhubarb Cream Pie is a delicious sample of the recipes from the Peoria, Illinois, sale.

In an enormous iron kettle, more volunteers brew hearty German-style borscht, filled with vegetables and chunks of beef. From another cauldron, moos, a sweet fruit soup, tempts passersby.

Early risers can sample more familiar fare at breakfast. The amateur short-order cooks of Buhler Mennonite Church sizzle German sausage that local butchers grind and flip 6,000 pancakes like pros. "It's fun!" Don Regier assures, as he piles hotcakes onto an endless line of waiting plates.

After breakfast, patrons hurry across the fairgrounds for a main attraction: the quilt auction. Some 300 painstakingly hand-sewn masterpieces await eager bidders. Time-proven patterns with fanciful names such as "Flower Garden" and "Sunbonnet Sue" share racks with new designs in daring paisleys.

By late afternoon, the quilt racks stand bare, and prices ranging from $225 to more than $3,000 add up to a total sale of $95,000.

For more moderately priced treasures, bargain hunters head for another building, where volunteers sell everything from plants grown in local gardens to cross-stitched tea towels. Nearby, the aroma of fresh bread beckons from open doors. Shoppers line up to buy homemade loaves, pies, and poppy-seed rolls.

An auction of crafts, antiques, and heirlooms lures visitors to another building. The auctioneer points to a

grandfather clock near the stage and relates its story:

Local craftsman Peter Lorentz planted a special walnut tree. Years later, Peter, now deceased, cut the tree down, built the clock in honor of his 50th wedding anniversary, and donated it to the sale. When the owner died, heirs donated the clock back to the auction.

Peter's nephew, Norman Wedel, of Moundridge, Kansas, proudly claims the clock for $3,500. "You have to think about where the money is going," Norman says. "And I decided this might be my last chance at one of my uncle's clocks."

Outside, crowds line a gravel road waiting for an unusual parade: the cattle walk. Volunteers and cows (about eight animals take turns) do 1-mile stints heading for the fairgrounds. Sponsors donate money for each of the 55 miles walked. Relishing the attention, young Jacob Miller of Inman coaxes a reluctant bovine toward the finish line. Jacob deserves the glory; he rounded up 90 sponsors for his mile and earned $400 for the sale.

As crowds dwindle, event president La Vern Stucky, a Peabody, Kansas, farmer, says he's almost sorry to see it end, but: "We're already planning for next year."

(Top) The fairgrounds livestock barn serves as the quilt auction house.
(Above) Wilma Diener's "Log Cabin Quilt" sold for $1,800.

133

Cream Cheese Brownies

This moist brownie comes from Lovell Franks in Peoria, Illinois. We added a chocolate frosting to the marbled top.

    3   ounces sweet baking chocolate
    3   tablespoons butter or margarine
    1   3-ounce package cream cheese,
          softened
    2   tablespoons butter or margarine
    ¼   cup sugar
    1   tablespoon all-purpose flour
    3   eggs
    1½ teaspoons vanilla
    ¾   cup sugar
    ⅛   teaspoon almond extract
    ½   cup all-purpose flour
    ½   teaspoon baking powder
    ¼   teaspoon salt
    ½   cup chopped nuts
          Chocolate Frosting (optional)

1. In a small heavy saucepan, melt sweet baking chocolate and the 3 tablespoons butter over low heat, stirring occasionally. Let cool.
2. For the cream cheese layer, in a small mixing bowl, beat together the cream cheese and 2 tablespoons butter till combined. Beat in the ¼ cup sugar, 1 tablespoon flour, *one* egg, and *½ teaspoon* vanilla till combined.
3. For chocolate layer, in another mixing bowl, beat together the ¾ cup sugar and *two* eggs. Beat in the melted and cooled chocolate, *1 teaspoon* vanilla, and the almond extract.
4. Add the ½ cup flour, baking powder, and salt, beating mixture just till combined. Stir in the nuts.
5. In a greased 9x9x2-inch baking pan, spread *half* of the chocolate mixture. Evenly spoon all of the cream cheese mixture over the chocolate layer, spreading evenly. Dollop remaining chocolate mixture over cream cheese layer. Swirl layers with a knife or spatula.
6. Bake in a 350° oven for 30 minutes. Cool in pan on a wire rack.
7. Frost brownies, if desired. Store, covered, in the refrigerator. Makes 16.
Chocolate Frosting: In a mixing bowl, beat together ½ cup sifted powdered sugar, 1 ounce melted and cooled *sweet baking chocolate*, and 1 tablespoon *butter* or *margarine* till smooth. Beat in 1½ cups sifted *powdered sugar* and enough *milk* (about 2 tablespoons) to make a spreadable frosting.

Bar Cookie Tip

To make freezing bar cookies easier, line a baking pan with foil before you begin a recipe. (Leave about 2 inches of foil above the edges of the pan.) When the bars have cooled, use the foil to lift the block of bars out of the pan. Place the uncut block in a freezer bag or container. Seal, label, and freeze. To use the bars, thaw them about 15 minutes.

Chewy Oat Cookies

Raisins and chocolate pieces flavor these cookies that Doris Christ of Elmwood, Illinois, bakes.

    ⅔   cup butter or margarine
    1⅓ cups packed brown sugar
    ⅓   cup peanut butter
    2   eggs
    1   teaspoon vanilla
    1   cup all-purpose flour
    ½   teaspoon baking soda
    ½   teaspoon baking powder
    ¼   teaspoon salt
    ½   cup buttermilk or sour milk
    2   cups regular or quick-cooking rolled
          oats
    1   cup wheat germ
    1   cup shelled sunflower seeds
    1   cup raisins
    1   6-ounce package (1 cup) semisweet
          chocolate pieces

1. In a mixing bowl, beat butter or margarine with an electric mixer for 30 seconds. Beat in the brown sugar and peanut butter till fluffy. Beat in eggs and vanilla.
2. In another mixing bowl combine flour, baking soda, baking powder, and salt. Add to beaten mixture alternately with buttermilk or sour milk.
3. Stir in the rolled oats, wheat germ, sunflower seeds, raisins, and chocolate.
4. Drop by tablespoonfuls onto ungreased cookie sheets. Bake in a 375° oven about 10 minutes or till golden brown. Remove from cookie sheets and cool on wire racks. Makes about 60 cookies.

(Clockwise from top) Cream Cheese Brownies, Peanut Butter Cookie Bars, Chewy Oat Cookies.

Half the fun at the sale is the camaraderie.

Peanut Butter Cookie Bars

Irresistible chocolate and peanut butter flavor these treats that Marie Litwiller of Hopedale, Illinois, bakes for the Peoria relief sale.

- ½ cup butter or *margarine*
- ½ cup peanut butter
- ½ cup sugar
- ½ cup packed brown sugar
- 1 egg
- 1 teaspoon vanilla
- 1 cup all-purpose flour
- ½ teaspoon baking soda
- ¼ teaspoon salt
- 1 cup quick-cooking rolled oats
- 1 6-ounce package (1 cup) semisweet chocolate pieces
  Peanut Butter Icing

1. In a mixing bowl, beat the butter or margarine and peanut butter with an electric mixer for 30 seconds. Add sugar and brown sugar. Beat till fluffy. Beat in the egg and vanilla.
2. Stir together the flour, baking soda, and salt. Add to the beaten mixture and beat till blended. Stir in the rolled oats.
3. Spread mixture into a 13x9x2-inch baking pan. Bake in a 350° oven for 20 minutes. Place pan on a wire rack. Sprinkle with chocolate. Let stand for 5 minutes. Spread chocolate over the surface. Cool.
4. Prepare icing. Drizzle over the chocolate layer. Cut into bars. Makes 30 to 36 cookies.
Peanut Butter Icing: In a bowl, beat together ¾ cup sifted *powdered sugar*, ¼ cup *creamy peanut butter*, and enough *milk* (2 to 3 tablespoons) to make an icing of drizzling consistency.

Verenika

Long lines of visitors form at the Kansas State Fairgrounds in Hutchinson for bowls of these cheese-filled dumplings.

- 2½ cups dry cottage cheese
- 2 eggs
  Dash pepper
- 3¾ cups all-purpose flour
- ⅓ cup nonfat dry milk powder
- ¾ teaspoon baking powder
- ½ teaspoon salt
- 2 beaten eggs
- ¾ cup water
- 4 teaspoons cooking oil
  Ham and Cream Gravy

1. For filling, in a blender container, combine cottage cheese, the first 2 eggs, and pepper. Cover and blend till smooth. Or beat with an electric mixer till smooth.
2. For dough, in a large mixing bowl, stir together flour, nonfat dry milk powder, baking powder, and salt.
3. In a small mixing bowl, beat together remaining 2 eggs, water, and cooking oil. Add to flour mixture and stir till combined. On a floured surface, knead dough about 10 strokes or till smooth.
4. Divide dough in half. Roll out each portion to ⅛-inch thickness. Using a 4-inch-round cutter (or a glass with a 3-inch-round opening), cut out rounds of dough. Place 1 tablespoon filling in the center of each circle. Moisten edge; fold over for a half moon. Pinch to seal. Reroll remaining dough.
5. In a large kettle or Dutch oven, cook dumplings in a large amount of boiling water, half at a time, about 7 minutes or till tender, stirring occasionally. Remove with a slotted spoon. Drain.
6. Serve dumplings with Ham and Cream Gravy. Makes 24 to 30.
Ham and Cream Gravy: In a medium saucepan, melt 3 tablespoons *butter or margarine*. Add 2 cups chopped fully cooked *ham* (12 ounces). Cook over medium heat till ham is light brown. Stir in 3 tablespoons all-purpose *flour*, ¼ teaspoon *salt*, and ⅛ teaspoon *pepper*. Add 2¼ cups *milk* all at once. Cook and stir over medium heat till thick and bubbly. Cook and stir for 1 minute more. Makes 3¼ cups.
To Use Your Microwave: Make Ham and Cream Gravy with the ingredients given above. In a 2-quart microwave-safe casserole, micro-cook butter, uncovered, on 100% power (high) for 40 to 60 seconds or till melted. Stir in flour, salt, and pepper. Stir in milk all at once. Cook, uncovered, on high for 7 to 9 minutes or till thickened and bubbly, stirring after every minute till thickened, then every 30 seconds. Stir in chopped ham. Cook for 1 to 2 minutes more or till heated through.

Verenika

Acknowledgments

Our special thanks to the following field editors, writers, photographers, and illustrators who contributed to this book.

Cover
Photographs: Mike Dieter (food) and
    Michael Vaughn.

Page 3
Photographs: Renee Byer and
    Dennis Cox.

Pages 4–8
Rosemary Hutchinson
Photographs: Dennis Cox,
    Wm. Hopkins, Jim Kascoutas,
    Barbara Martin, Perry Struse,
    Al Teufen, and Tony Walsh.
Illustration: Thomas Rosborough.

Pages 10–21
State Fair Winners: Blue Ribbon Recipes
Peggy Ammerman, Charlyn Fargo,
    and Diana McMillen.
Photographs: Mike Dieter (food),
    Wm. Hopkins, Perry Struse, and
    Michael Vaughan.

Pages 22–31
Harvest Time in Cranberry Country
George Hendrix.
Photographs: Mike Dieter (food)
    and Wm. Hopkins.

Pages 32–40
*A Harvest of Good Eating
And Great Fun: Sweet Corn*
Alan Guebert.
Photographs: Mike Dieter (food) and
    Michael Vaughn.

Pages 42–50
*Great Times, Good Eating
At the Old Apple Orchard*
Pat Westfall.
Photographs: Mike Dieter (food) and
    Wm. Hopkins.

Pages 51–53
Nuts to You from Iowa
Amy Elbert.
Photographs: Mike Dieter (food)
    and Jim Kascoutas.

Pages 54–64
Bring on the Berries: Sweet Pickin's
Roger Drayna and George Hendrix.
Photographs: Mike Dieter (food),
    Wm. Hopkins, and Rob Orcutt.

Pages 63–65
Harvesting a North Woods Delicacy
Dale Ortman.
Photographs: Mike Dieter (food)
    and Jack Renduluch.

Pages 66–67
North Dakota Sunflower Sensations
Diana McMillen.
Photograph: Mike Dieter.

Pages 68–69
Tasty Fixin's from an Ozark Kitchen
Diana McMillen and Steve Slack.
Photograph: Mike Dieter (food) and
    Perry Struse.

Pages 70–72
Stalking the Elusive Morel
Sara Gay and Tom Dammann.
Photograph: John R. Shibley.

Pages 74–81
Best of the Wursts
Rebecca Christian, Barbara Delhotal,
    and George Hendrix.
Photographs: Bob Barrett,
    Mike Dieter (food), Mitch Hrdlicka,
    and Barbara Martin.

Pages 82–91
*Yuletide Favorites from the Old Country:
Baker's Choice*

Mary Gunderson, George Hendrix,
    Martin Hintz, and
    Katherine Rodeghier.
Photographs: Todd Dacquisto,
    Susan Gilmore, Wm. Hopkins,
    and Scott Little.

Pages 92–101
Stone-Ground Goodness
Diana McMillen.
Photographs: Bob Barrett,
    Mike Dieter (food),
    Connie Girard, and Wm. Hopkins.

Pages 102–108
From Midwest Candy Shops: Sweet Secrets
Kathleen Flood, Mary Gunderson,
    and Jane Ware.
Photographs: Mike Dieter (food),
    Connie Girard, Paul Jones,
    and Barbara Martin.

Pages 110–113
Fresh-from-the-Farm Goodness
Jan Riggenbach.
Photographs: Renee Byer, Dennis Cox,
    and Todd Dacquisto.

Pages 114–124
*Fresh Flavors and Aromas
From City Markets*
Peggy Ammerman,
    Sarah Crump Brown, and
    Lynn Hoppe Phelps.
Photographs: Mike Dieter (food),
    Eric Hanson, Barbara Martin,
    and Michael Vaughn.

Pages 124–137
*Old-Country Foods and Flavors
From Midwest Mennonite Communities*
Barbara Briggs Morrow.
Photographs: Mike Dieter (food)
    and Larry Fleming.

Page 138
Photograph: Bob Barrett

State Index

Illinois

Apple picking, 44
Aunt Anna Ulrich's Rolls, 130
Best-Ever Raisin-Orange Bread, 15
Bountiful Corn Stir-Fry, 38
Bread baking, Monmouth, 13
Chewy Oat Cookies, 134
Chocolate Frosting, 134
Corn festivals, 33, 35
Corn-Tomato Relish, 40
Corny Corn Bread, 40
Cream-Cheese Brownies, 134
Grilled Ham and Corn Kabobs, 39
Hoopeston
    National Sweet Corn Festival, 33
Market, Princeton, 110
Mennonite Relief Auction, Peoria, 132
Monmouth
    bread baking, 13
National Sweet Corn Festival,
    Hoopeston, 33
Orange Glaze, 16
Pastry for Single-Crust Pie, 130
Peanut Butter Cookie Bars, 136
Peanut Butter Icing, 136
Peoria
    Mennonite Relief Auction, 132
Peoria Rhubarb Cream Pie, 130
Puffy Skillet Corn Fritters, 38
Princeton market, 110
Raisin-Lovers' Surprise Loaves, 16
Spicy Corn-Stuffed Tomato Salad, 39
State Fair, 13
Sunrise Serenade Coffee Cake, 16
Walnut Glaze, 16

Indiana

Apple picking, 44
Cherry-Berry Surprise Pie, 20
City Market, Indianapolis, 123
Corn festival, 35
Greenfield
    pie baking, 10
Helen Rushton's Make-Ahead
    Piecrust, 21
Indianapolis City Market, 123
John Walker's Hash-Brown
    Quiche, 122
Market
    City Market, Indianapolis, 123

Markleville
    pie baking, 10
Mary Alice Collins' Old-Fashioned
    Lard Piecrust, 21
Meringue, 20
Old Faithful Sugar-Cream Pie, 20
Pasticcio with Kima, 124
Pie baking, Greenfield, 10
Pride-o'-the-Fair Chocolate Pie, 20
State Fair, 10

Iowa

Apple picking, 44
Bakery
    Sykora Bakery, Cedar Rapids, 90
Cedar Rapids
    Sykora Bakery, 90
Chocolate-on-Chocolate Walnut
    Cookies, 53
Chunky Cherry-Cobbler Ice Cream, 18
Cobbler Topping, 18
Corn festivals, 35
Ellston
    ice cream making, 12
Ice cream making, 12
Judges' Choice German-Chocolate
    Ice Cream, 18
Marville's Marvelous Maple-Nut
    Ice Cream, 53
Nutting, 51
Perry
    nutting, 51
Ripe 'n' Rich Black Raspberry
    Ice Cream, 19
State Fair, 12
Sykora Bakery, Cedar Rapids, 90
Sykora's Vaňočka, 90
Walnuts, 51

Kansas

Apple picking, 45
Cookie Glaze, 130
Ham and Cream Gravy, 136
Hutchinson
    Mennonite Relief Auction, 126
Hutchinson Beef Borscht, 128
Kauffmans' Apple Butter, 126
Mennonite Relief Auction,
    Hutchinson, 126
New Year's Cookies, 130
Roepke Processing Plant,
    Waterville, 78

Sausage
    Roepke Processing Plant,
        Waterville, 78
Sausage and Mostaccioli Bake, 79
Sausage-Wild Rice Casserole, 80
Verenika, 136
Waterville
    Roepke Processing Plant, 78

Michigan

Apple Pastry Squares, 49
Apple picking, 42, 45
Apple Pudding with Rummy Sauce, 49
Bakery
    Dutch Delite Pastry Shop,
        Holland, 86
Bavarian Honey-Bran Muffins, 94
Blueberry-Cream Cheese Fingers, 57
Blueberry picking, 54
Blueberry-Sour Cream Cake, 56
Brandied Apple Roll-Ups, 46
Chicken with Morel Cream Sauce, 72
Chunky Applesauce, 46
DeGrandchamp Blueberry Farm,
    South Haven, 54
Detroit
    Eastern Market, 110
Dutch Delite Bankets, 87
Dutch Delite Butterdough, 86
Dutch Delite Krakeling, 87
Dutch Delite Pastry Shoppe,
    Holland, 86
Eau Claire
    apple picking, 42
Eastern Market, Detroit, 110
Frankenmuth Mill, 93
Fruit picking
    apples, Eau Claire, 42
    blueberries, South Haven, 54
Glazed Fresh Apple Cookies, 47
Grandma Teichman's Apple
    Dressing, 46
Holland
    Dutch Delite Pastry Shoppe, 86
Icing, 87
Market
    Eastern Market, Detroit, 110
Milk Chocolate Blueberry Clusters, 56
Mill, Frankenmuth, 93
Mini Crepes, 48
Morels, 70
Morel-Zucchini Frittata, 72
Mushroom hunting, 70
Powdered Sugar Icing, 49
Quick-Fix Corn Sticks, 93
Rummy Sauce, 49

Recipe Index

A-B

Almond Toffee, 108
Apples
  Apple Pastry Squares, 49
  Apple Pie á la
    Mode, 50
  Apple Pudding with Rummy
    Sauce, 49
  Brandied Apple Roll-Ups, 46
  Chunky Applesauce, 46
  Cranberry-Apple-Nut Pie, 30
  Glazed Fresh Apple
    Cookies, 47
  Grandma Teichman's Apple
    Dressing, 46
  The Kauffmans' Apple Butter, 126
Applesauce Cake, Rita's, 99
Aunt Anna Ulrich's Rolls, 130
Bavarian Honey-Bran Muffins, 94
Beef
  Hutchinson Beef Borscht, 128
  Pasticcio with Kima, 124
Best-Ever Raisin-Orange Bread, 15
Blueberries
  Blueberry-Cream Cheese Fingers, 57
  Blueberry-Sour Cream Cake, 56
  Milk Chocolate Blueberry
    Clusters, 54
  White Blueberry Clusters, 54
Blue-Ribbon Cranberry Chicken, 31
Bountiful Corn Stir-Fry, 38
Brandied Apple Roll-Ups, 46
Bran Muffins, Bavarian Honey-, 94
Breads, Quick
  Bavarian Honey-Bran Mufffins, 94
  Brownville Corn Pancakes, 96
  Chippewa Muffins, 65
  Corny Corn Bread, 40
  Puffy Skillet Corn Fritters, 38
  Quick-Fix Corn Sticks, 93
Breads, Yeast
  Aunt Anna Ulrich's Rolls, 130
  Best-Ever Raisin-Orange Bread, 15
  New Year's Cookies, 130
  Raisin-Lovers' Suprise Loaves, 16
  Sunrise Serenade Coffee Cake, 16
  Sykora's Vaňočka, 90
  Van's Cranberry Fritters, 26
Brownies, Cream Cheese, 134
Brownville Corn Pancakes, 96
Butterscotch Filling, 89

C-D

Cabbage
  German Skillet Supper, 80
  Hutchinson Beef Borscht, 128
Cakes
  Blueberry-Sour Cream Cake, 56
  Rita's Applesauce Cake, 99
  Vanilla Nut Cake, 120
Candies
  Almond Toffee, 108
  Caramels, 103
  Chocolate Truffles, 108
  Hard Candy, 103
  Heavenly Hash, 106
  Milk Chocolate Blueberry
    Clusters, 56
  Mint-Chocolate Truffles, 108
  Orange-Chocolate Truffles, 108
  Sauerkraut Candy, 106
  White Blueberry Clusters, 56
Caramels, 103
Casseroles
  Celebration Casserole, 65
  John Walker's Hash-Brown
    Quiche, 122
  Pasticcio with Kima, 124
  Sausage and Mostaccioli Bake, 79
  Sausage Soufflé, 75
  Sausage-Wild Rice Casserole, 80
Celebration Casserole, 65
Cheese
  Jerabek's Cheese Tarts, 83
  John Walker's Hash-Brown
    Quiche, 122
  Pasticcio with Kima, 124
  Sausage and Mostaccioli Bake, 79
  Sausage Soufflé, 75
  Strawberries in Petal Cups, 61
  Verenika, 136
Cherry-Berry Surprise Pie, 20
Cherry-Cobbler Ice Cream, Chunky, 18
Chewy Oat Cookies, 134
Chicken
  Blue-Ribbon Cranberry Chicken, 31
  Chicken with Morel Cream
    Sauce, 72
  Poulet au Vin Blanc, 118
  Sausage-Wild Rice Casserole, 80
Chippewa Muffins, 65
Chocolate
  Almond Toffee, 108
  Chewy Oat Cookies, 134
  Chocolate Frosting, 134
  Chocolate-on-Chocolate Walnut
    Cookies, 53
  Chocolate Truffles, 108

Chocolate (continued)
  Cranberry Candy-Bar Cookies, 27
  Cream Cheese Brownies, 134
  Heavenly Hash, 106
  Judges' Choice German-Chocolate
    Ice Cream, 18
  Milk Chocolate Blueberry Clusters, 56
  Mint-Chocolate Truffles, 108
  Orange-Chocolate Truffles, 108
  Peanut Butter Cookie Bars, 136
  Pride-o'-the Fair Chocolate Pie, 20
Chunky Applesauce, 46
Chunky Cherry-Cobbler Ice Cream, 18
Citified Greens, 68
Cobbler Topping, 18
Coconut
  Judges' Choice German-Chocolate
    Ice Cream, 18
  Sauerkraut Candy, 106
Coffee Cakes
  O & H Kringle, 89
  Sunrise Serenade Coffee Cake, 16
Cooked Wild Rice, 65
Cookie Glaze, 130
Cookies
  Chewy Oat Cookies, 134
  Chocolate-on-Chocolate Walnut
    Cookies, 53
  Cranberry Candy-Bar Cookies, 27
  Cream Cheese Brownies, 134
  Crunchy Cornmeal Cookies, 100
  Dutch Delite Krakeling, 87
  Glazed Fresh Apple Cookies, 47
  Harold's Health Cookies, 98
  Jerabek's Cheese Tarts, 83
  Jerabek's Linzer Cookies, 83
  New Year's Cookies, 130
  Peanut Butter Cookie Bars, 136
  Sun Crunchies, 67
Corn
  Bountiful Corn Stir-Fry, 38
  Corn-Tomato Relish, 40
  Corny Corn Bread, 40
  Grilled Ham and Corn Kabobs, 39
  Puffy Skillet Corn Fritters, 38
  Spicy Corn-Stuffed Tomato
    Salad, 38
Cornmeal
  Brownville Corn Pancakes, 96
  Corny Corn Bread, 40
  Crunchy Cornmeal Cookies, 100
  Quick-Fix Corn Sticks, 93
Corny Corn Bread, 40
Cranberries
  Blue-Ribbon Cranberry Chicken, 31
  Cranberry-Apple-Nut Pie, 30
  Cranberry Candy-Bar Cookies, 27
  Frosted Cranberries, 30
  Van's Cranberry Fritters, 26
  Winner's-Circle Salad, 30

S-Z

Have *Midwest Living*
magazine delivered to your
door. For information, write to:
Midwest Living
Magazine Customer Service
P.O. Box 52971
Boulder, CO 80322-2971
or call toll-free: 1-800-374-9378